Anger Management 101
For Men & Women

CLIVE WOLFE

Text Copyright © Clive Wolfe

All rights reserved. No part of this guide may be reproduced in any form without permission in writing from the publisher except in the case of brief quotations embodied in critical articles or reviews.

Legal & Disclaimer

The information contained in this book and its contents is not designed to replace or take the place of any form of medical or professional advice; and is not meant to replace the need for independent medical, financial, legal or other professional advice or services, as may be required. The content and information in this book have been provided for educational and entertainment purposes only.

The content and information contained in this book have been compiled from sources deemed reliable, and it is accurate to the best of the Author's knowledge, information, and belief. However, the Author cannot guarantee its accuracy and validity and cannot be held liable for any errors and/or omissions. Further, changes are periodically made to this book as and when needed. Where appropriate and/or necessary, you must consult a professional (including but not limited to your doctor, attorney, financial advisor or such other professional advisor) before using any of the suggested remedies, techniques, or information in this book.

Upon using the contents and information contained in this book, you agree to hold harmless the Author from and against any damages, costs, and expenses, including any legal fees potentially resulting from the application of any of the information provided by this book. This disclaimer applies to any loss, damages or injury caused by the use and application, whether directly or indirectly, of any advice or information presented, whether for breach of contract, tort, negligence, personal injury, criminal intent, or under any other cause of action.

You agree to accept all risks of using the information presented inside this book.

You agree that by continuing to read this book, where appropriate and/or necessary, you shall consult a professional (including but not limited to your doctor, attorney, or financial advisor or such other advisor as needed) before using any of the suggested remedies, techniques, or information in this book.

Contents

Introduction 1

Chapter 1: The Reaction of Our Body When We Feel Angry 5

    The Busy Body 6

        Glands 6

        Hormones 7

        Brain 8

        Heart and Body 10

Chapter 2: Stress Management 13

    Major Causes of Stress 16

Chapter 3: Anger in Childhood 22

    Emotional Development in Children 22

    How to Deal with an Angry Child 30

    Dealing with Angry Teenagers 34

Chapter 4: Different Types of Anger 39

    Painful Emotions 39

Chapter 5: Is Anger the Same for Men and Women? 52

Neural Wiring in Men and Women............52

Hormonal Differences in Men and Women 56

Social Differences in Men and Women.......60

Chapter 6: Identifying Anger Issues................63

Self-Harming 65

Road Rage...68

Where to get help for Anger Management.76

Chapter 7: Lifestyle Changes 78

Dietary Needs...78

Exercise 81

Sleep 83

Chapter 8: Anger Management Techniques & Exercises...91

Help from Others 91

Self Help...96

Chapter 9: Domestic Violence........................110

Poverty and Familial Violence 110

Causes of Anger in Relationships..............113

Chapter 10: Manipulation and Anger 123

Narcissistic Personality Disorder (NPD)...124

Chapter 11: The Importance of Empathy 132

    Empathic Anger Management (EAM).......133

Chapter 12: There is a Good Side to Anger...142

    Turn Your Anger Into a Useful Tool..........142

Chapter 13: Becoming a Good person 150

    Forgiveness 152

    Sacrifice..154

    Being Non-judgmental................................156

Chapter 14: Maintaining Equilibrium in your Life 158

    Alternative Responding Mechanisms........160

    Don't be a quitter!..163

Chapter 15: Natural Healing 166

Conclusion 172

Introduction

Are you in denial of your anger outbursts?

Anger is not unique to specific people; it's something we all feel from time to time. That's because it's a normal emotion to experience. For some, an angry outburst may be linked to stress and frustration. When anger becomes aggressive or violent, it becomes a problem. If this sounds like you or someone you know, then this book will help you. You will learn to help yourself or someone you know on how to take control of uncontrolled anger.

This is a guide to show you how an aggressively angry person can successfully turn their life around. Aggression is not something we inherit by nature, but it's linked to certain experiences that happen to us throughout our lives. If you can identify your trigger points, then you can begin to heal yourself. Note the phrase "heal." The psychologist's bible, The Diagnostic and Statistical Manual of Mental Disorders (DSM) has an entry for uncontrolled anger bursts. They call it

Intermittent explosive disorder (IED), and it's a recognized psychological illness.

It is easy to understand how those of us who are victims of bad or no parenting can end up with psychological issues. Not that everyone can use that as an excuse for bad behavior, but sadly, studies do link poor parenting with maladaptive behavior in adults. Of course, some have the fortitude and strength of character to rise above an unhappy childhood. However, most will suffer some consequences and often that can show as uncontrollable anger.

This is a book that will guide you on how to turn negative thought patterns into positive ones and how to gain a mindset that can, and will, lead you on the road to success. Success can be measured in many ways. For those who have lost loving relationships through their violent behavior, their triumph will be in rebuilding such social connections.

Allow us to show you how to find your place in society; it's a place that's hidden because of your anger issues. The knowledge you will acquire in this book will open your eyes. There is so much you can't see just because you are blinded with a negative thinking pattern. Everyone is capable of becoming a better person. For you, it will be defined by a renewed understanding of life.

Learn how to see arguments from others' perspective. We will show you how to change your personality from cold and frightening to warm and friendly.

If you're the victim of an aggressively angry person, learn how to help them. Show them how to rid themselves of the bad and ugly thoughts that riddle them with distress. It can be done through professional therapy or using our self-help guide. Such people need to learn about who they are and how they play a vital role in this world.

Now is the time for action!

No one wants to live a lonely life because of uncontrollable anger. Once you read the contents of these pages, you will know the new direction your life must take.

Many of the ideas in this book are based on long-term studies that have proven to be successful in helping to control aggressive reactions. Being known as an angry person can only be detrimental to your very existence. Instead, learn how to show friendship and compassion to those who pass through your life.

Don't waste another day of your life!

Chapter 1

THE REACTION OF OUR BODY WHEN WE FEEL ANGRY

What comes to mind when you think of the word "anger?"

- ❖ Fighting
- ❖ Shouting
- ❖ Pushing and shoving
- ❖ Blood and Tears
- ❖ Abusive language and fast actions
- ❖ Assault

None of these descriptions portray a comfortable situation and often repulse most of us. Yet, the emotion of anger could save your life as it is one of the emotions that can trigger the "fight or flight" response. This natural biological reaction is essential should we find ourselves confronted by danger. Anger is an emotion that can be difficult to control, but it is possible to regulate the outcome of such a powerful feeling.

Emotional regulation is all about science, or rather about biochemicals. If we understand what's going on in our body, we may find that we're more equipped to regulate anger as well as other emotions, such as stress and depression.

We come to understand in adulthood that our thoughts and actions are ruled by the production of hormones. Such chemicals are produced from various glands around our body. They then make their way to the brain.

The Busy Body

Glands

You might ask, "What has anger got to do with my glands?"

If you know what your glands are doing in your body, you will be better able to control the chemical reactions.

These are the hormones that are making you feel angry and stressed.

There are many glands in our body, and they also vary between men and women. For instance, a woman has a gland that helps to trigger milk for her baby. Men have glands that produce testosterone, which triggers hair growth. There are glands that secrete chemicals into our bloodstream and glands that help us secrete sweat.

Hormones

The hormone we produce most of all when stressed is cortisol. Yet, when we're angry, cortisol production decreases. The hormone that increases in production is testosterone, for both males and females. The sudden increase in testosterone gives us a huge increase in energy. Adrenaline is also increased. This provides us with hormonal arousal that can last for days. That's why you can't always calm down after the situation that ignited your anger is over. Often, we remain irritable after an angry phase, such as an argument with someone. We can also find that for a few days, we can't concentrate very well. That's all thanks to our hormonal production from the glands.

Brain

The brain is our main control center, a place most of our nerves are connected to, hence the name "neuro." Within the brain is a network of transmitters, hence they are called neurotransmitters. Imagine them as little nerve-portals. Most of what we experience is processed in the brain, which then sends messages to the rest of our body.

Whilst the brain is a complex organ, it can help if you think of it as a computer system, with sectional areas.

- ❖ There is a part of the brain called the "cortex." This is where our logic and thinking processes happen. It is our strategic center.
- ❖ Another part of the brain is the emotional center, known as the "limbic." This is actually a primitive part of our brain. When we begin to feel anger, we are using the "limbic" section

more than we are using the cortex. That's why you can't think clearly when you are angry.

- ❖ The final section to include in our analysis is a small department within the "limbic" section. In there, you will find a warehouse full of your memories. This is the "amygdala." Some even refer to it as a reptilian feature. It is here where information passes through to go either to the cortex or the limbic. If the "amygdala" senses a strong sense of negative emotion, it sends it directly to the limbic. This means that the information bypasses the logical thinking of the cortex area. There is even a name for this process; it's called the "amygdala hijacking."

We can blame our anger on "amygdala hijacking." This process will trigger hormones and send our metabolic system into override. As the glands start transmitting adrenalin to the brain, the brain is busy redirecting the main blood flow from the gut to the muscles. We now have biochemical changes going on inside our body. Basically, it means our energy is being redirected to our muscles. We're about to explode with inner tension.

Such metabolic changes then start to affect other parts of our body too.

Heart and Body

Two crucial organs in your body are affected by anger, they are the brain and heart. The heart will pump faster. The brain will redirect energy in the bloodstream from the gut to the muscles. Ever got that churning feeling in your gut that something isn't quite right? That's because of the bio-reactions in the heart and brain. This can cause raised blood pressure. Then you will have a higher temperature, and you will need to breath faster for oxygen relief. You may perspire more in those moments and your mind will be sharper for a while, as you deal with your response.

It is all a similar process to when you feel anxious or stressed. Given all that's happening inside your body, you can see why a prolonged course of these metabolic changes could make you unwell. Considering the results of such negative emotions, it's no surprise that the immune system is weakened and you may suffer any of the following:

- ❖ Headaches or possible bad migraines.
- ❖ Digestive upsets that can lead to heartburn or conditions such as Irritable Bowel Syndrome (IBS).
- ❖ High blood pressure, which weakens the circulatory system making you more prone to heart disease or strokes.
- ❖ Surprisingly, you will also be more sensitive to pain, which is the last thing you want if you're forced to fight instead of flight.
- ❖ You are also less able to cope with inflammation in your joints and muscles so you may feel achy.

Anger, just like stress and anxiety, is an emotion. It is an emotion that triggers fear and excitement. As you pass through the unsettled responses of the emotion, you need to learn how to deal with your inner feelings. Only then can you reduce the risk of becoming aggressive or violent.

- ❖ The word anger does not mean the same as the word violence. Anger is an emotion.
- ❖ Violence is not an emotion; it is a reaction.

Why then do some people lose their tempers openly and become violent? Then there are others who consider their anger to be a bad emotion, and so they try to hide it. We all have different coping mechanisms in place.

Let's now leave behind the responses of the body. We will move on to consider at what point in our lives our anger becomes uncontrollable.

Chapter 2

STRESS MANAGEMENT

Emotions

Many of our feelings are based on one or more of the main six emotions we experience on a daily basis:

1. Happiness
2. Surprise
3. Anger
4. Disgust
5. Fear
6. Sadness

Some believe there are more, but our feelings can fall in-between or be a combination of any of these main categories, such as:

- ❖ Confusion could be fear and surprise.
- ❖ Envy could be disgust and anger.
- ❖ Anxiety could fall anywhere but happiness.

Then again, one emotion can stem from the other, such as anger can be a result of fear.

What makes one person happy may fill someone one else with fear, such as skydiving or other high adrenaline sports.

Every thought we have and every sense we feel in our minds are all related to our emotions. It can be difficult to navigate around the constant stream of thoughts in our heads in any one day. That's why you need to learn to take control. This is never truer if you suffer stress every day of your life.

Stress can fall under anger, fear, and even sadness, as it leads us into a depression. It's a strong emotion that can have negative effects on your wellbeing if you suffer for an excessive length of time. If we overindulge in stress, we are more likely to suffer anger. Once again, it results in too much production of stress-related hormones. After all, the natural chemicals in our body have an effect on every cell we produce.

Some researchers believe that we broadcast and receive vibrations from each other. This is carried out through our electrochemical receptors. They theorize that humans generate vibes like an electromagnetic field. It's no surprise then, how fear can spread like wildfire as a wave of panic through a group of people. Likewise, stress and anger can be passed among the members of a family.

Yet, it is such emotions that help us survive. Anger is a call to defend ourselves. Stress is closely related. Both of which can cause us harm, if we experience them for too long.

When the chemicals react inside us, they send signals out to our blood cells. It takes only 6 seconds to inform the whole body of a new emotion. If we wish to continue feeling that way, we choose on an unconscious level to prolong the feeling. You'd think that we would only choose good feelings, but some enjoy fear, such as adrenalin junkies.

Major Causes of Stress

A major cause of stress in the US is, surprise surprise, money. We all strive to pay the rent and, bills and put food on the table because these are our fundamental priorities. We need shelter and sustenance to survive. Money is not the only cause of stress; here are a few other top reasons:

- Financial commitments.
- Separation from a loved one because of death or divorce.
- Getting married.
- Moving home.
- Illnesses.
- Difficulties at work.

Then there are environmental factors, such as living with a person who makes you unhappy, particularly if they are violent. Living with constant worry can lead to depression and anxiety.

Common Symptoms of Stress

- Chest pains or palpitations.

- ❖ Feeling excessively hot or cold, often with shivers.
- ❖ Eating too much for comfort, or not enough because of loss of appetite.
- ❖ High blood pressure, which can lead to heart disease if prolonged.
- ❖ Muscle pains through constant tension.
- ❖ Headaches.
- ❖ Sleeping difficulties.
- ❖ Digestive problems.

If you suffer stress, you are more likely to be snappy and short tempered. Your moods could lead to feeling annoyed and angry with everyone. You may say or do things that you wouldn't normally say, such as shouting at the children. Then you live with the regret afterward. Stress can also lead to the overuse of alcohol or non-prescribed drugs as you seek an escape route. However, all this does is add to your problems.

If this sounds familiar and you are experiencing these symptoms, then it's time to take control. Bring your life back into balance. You can begin with a little self-healing, but you should seek help from others too. As with any lifestyle change, it begins with you.

Here are a few ideas to consider introducing into your life:

❖ If you're drinking too much alcohol, allow yourself to drink it only on certain days of the week. Try and have at least three days when you do not consume any alcohol at all. Drinking excessively can make you lose control, particularly if you have a lower anger threshold. You will lose all inhibitions, and that will only make you more aggressive. There are also effects on the next day, making you will feel lethargic and short-tempered in the morning. This is no good if you need to get to work. Try drinking on your days off, such as the weekend only. If you can't control your intake of alcohol, then do get professional help as soon as possible because things will only get worse. Look online for a local Alcoholics Anonymous (AA) group, or ask at a chemist or clinic for details. There, you will meet other sufferers, and you can come together to help each other.

- If you're worried that you're overeating for comfort, write down some meal plans for three meals a day. Include healthy snacks such as peanuts, raisins, yogurts, or fruit. You can eat these in-between meals, so you don't feel hungry. Make a shopping list of the meals and only buy what's on the list. Try not to go down the candy aisle or the bakery area when you're in the superstore. The aroma will tempt you to buy those unhealthy items.
- You can also try writing down everything you eat in a day. You might be shocked to see how much comfort eating you're doing.
- Doing activities such as the ones suggested here will force you to think about the food you're eating. Often we eat with an automatic urgency giving no thought to what we're putting in our mouths. The next time to you eat something, chew on the food for longer. Try to make the meal last 20 minutes because this is the time it takes the receptors in your brain to know when

you are full. Think about the flavors and textures. This will stop automatic eating for the sake of it. Keep the naughty carb treats for only one day in the week. Research "nutrition" online. There is a lot of useful information about which foods are the healthiest.

❖ If your finances are in a poor condition, then you must seek help and advice. Swallow your pride and admit that you can't keep up with the bills. If your income doesn't meet your outgoings, then it's time to make cutbacks on things such as energy bills, food, clothing but most importantly, on luxury items, such as phones and computers. Sit down and write down every single bill you have so it's clear in your mind as you look at the figures. See where you can make realistic cutbacks. Contact the companies that you owe money to and explain that you can't afford the present amount and need to cut it down. Put your bills in order of importance, with the roof over your head and your food as a top priority.

- ❖ As you can see from these suggestions, it's all about thinking clearly and admitting you have a problem. You must look at ways of resolving those problems.
- ❖ The first person you must care for is yourself. If you are not healthy, then you can't keep your family safe and happy. Try to get more exercise into your life because that costs nothing but can be a great cure for a troubled mind and body. Walks are great stress busters, but not on busy streets. Head to a peaceful place, such as a park. Make sure that every week you're doing something for yourself that you enjoy. We all need a break from the fast pace of life, so give yourself a break to reboot yourself for the rest of the week.

Chapter 3

ANGER IN CHILDHOOD

Emotional Development in Children

We are not born angry. Babies cry for attention, but that is an innate instinct and not anger. At what point in our childhood then does anger manifest itself? We know that babies can feel happy because they laugh. Whilst none of us remember much in the way of our baby years, they are busy years as we soak-in everything that's going on around us.

It's argued that some emotions are innate in babies. These are happiness, disgust, and distress. Babies display these emotions through body posture and facial expressions. Other emotions develop over time and become recognized milestones, as outlined below. Some develop quicker or slower than others, but all are normal in a baby's emotional growth.

Baby Steps

4 months - babies can identify certain facial expressions in the faces that look down at them. If it's a smile, the baby might feel happy and smile back.

6 months – babies will mimic those around them more and more. If there's a baby crying, another baby may cry too. If they hear laughter, they may join in.

8-9 months - babies now recognize their main carer and begin to experience anxiety when they're not around. They are now developing emotions that they begin to find uncomfortable. Some may cry out loud in protest, such as with separation anxiety. Others may simply whimper, not quite sure how to handle the new feelings. This is generally regarded as our first emotional rock.

11-12 months – smiling back at someone who smiles at them is no longer automatic. The baby is now associating which feelings go with which expression. It's a trigger of cognitive processes of working things out for themselves.

15-18 months – emotions can begin to overwhelm a baby as they learn the feelings of frustration. Now they're starting to demonstrate their frustrations, possibly even with tantrums. Is this the beginning of anger?

21-months – this is when they start to make conscious decisions. They might be willing to share their toys, then again they might not. Our personality is starting to shine through.

2 years – now that we know how to playact with our emotions, we might pretend-cry so we can get our own way. At this point, humans begin to experience empathy. If we take our playmates' toy and they cry, we have a good idea what's caused them to cry. What we do about it depends on how our own personality is developing.

Do our anger issues begin as a sort of baby frustration? A baby cries to get attention. If no attention is forthcoming, a baby is likely to become confused and start crying louder. Is this the festering of our uncontrollable emotions taking over? What we experience around us at a young age molds our personality.

One such study by Brooker et al. in 2014 tested infants aged 6-12 months to examine anger issues in infants. Parents filled in a questionnaire. This was designed to measure the stability of home-life. It enabled them to identify if any of a set of ten stressful life events had occurred within the family. The infants underwent a process to measure how they reacted to a mildly stressful experience.

The initial results were interesting, in that differences between genders became obvious. The boys showed their frustrations sooner than the girls. Each child's reactions were measured and given a low or high anger profile.

At 3 years of age, the parents were given a second questionnaire. Those measured with a high anger profile went on to be more problematic with their behavior. One prevalent factor that high-anger profilers shared was the amount of stress in their home environment. This indicated that early childhood stresses could be a cause of problematic behavior in later development.

Another study highlighted what effect maternal relationships have on infants. Those that have had a better maternal relationship seem to develop fewer psychological problems.

Mental Health Issues in Children

There have been various researches on the behavior of children over the years. Given that anger is an emotion that even an adult finds difficult to control, it can be tenfold for a child. The most important rule any adult can have is not to lose their temper with a child who is throwing a tantrum. They are experiencing an uncontrollable outburst and need help, not hindrance.

Anger issues in children can go hand in hand with certain mental illness conditions:

Obsessive Compulsive Disorders (OCD)

This is when a child suffers anxious moments on a regular basis. It can then lead to the formation of obsessive behavior. Such behavior can easily turn into a ritual in their lives. If they cannot carry out their ritual, they risk becoming over-anxious, which can lead to an outburst of anger.

Attention Deficit Hyperactivity Disorder (ADHD)

This illness affects the ability of a child to focus and concentrate. Their minds become overactive, and it can lead to the child becoming noisy and disruptive. A child with ADHD can also be quite impatient. Unable to wait for their turn in a line, or wait for anything at all, can lead to difficulties with their peers.

Tourette's Syndrome

It's a form of motor and vocal tics, such as fast-blinking eyes or making loud grunting sounds. The more stressed the child becomes, the more tics and louder their noises. As they develop into teenagers, they can become obsessed with words that may offend. Their deviance is the outlet for stress.

Autism

This can slow down a child's natural social development. In turn, that causes difficulties with communicating and learning. Frustration will be quick to set in and can lead to an outburst of outrageous behavior.

Just like medical conditions, anger issues can be connected to a child's environment and experiences:

Dysfunctional Family

What is happening at home plays a large role in a child's development. If they have an unstable home life where little guidance is forthcoming, the child may have not learned what good behavior is. Or, they may have been allowed to get away with anger outbursts because no one cared to control them. It could be the only way they can defend themselves from abusive parents or siblings.

Parental Behavior

This is the most important role model for a child. If the people they love and trust have constant outbursts of shouting or violence, they may believe this is the norm. Equally, if the parents believe in harmful punishments for bad behavior, this may be a cause for poor development.

Neglect

Even a child from a dysfunctional family can be happy if shown guidance by their parents. If a child suffers at the hands of abusive parents or family members, they will most likely develop anger issues that they have to keep internal.

Traumatic Events

Children can suffer Post Traumatic Stress Disorder (PTSD) if they have a bad experience. Once stress and depression set in, the child will become unbalanced emotionally.

If your child is still pre-school age, they may still grow out of the tantrum stage, most especially once they discover their peer groups don't like it. If their angry behavior continues once they start their school education, this is a warning signal. You may find their teachers suggesting a psychological evaluation. Any parent who is having problems with their child's behavior should welcome this invitation. There is no shame in helping your child to cope with the difficulties that life can throw their way.

How to Deal with an Angry Child

At an early age, anger issues tend to be related to frustration. In infants, it could be something as simple as not getting their own way. After all, we see to a baby's every need when they cry, so it makes sense that toddlers don't understand why that should change. They are now experiencing how to deal with the anxieties of life. When an infant displays frustration through anger, they need the help of an adult to guide them through these new confusing emotions.

Most importantly, as their carer, you should:

- ❖ **Look for the trigger points** so you can plan ahead. Has their usual routine been altered, thus causing them stress? Learn to recognize what is upsetting your child's emotions to the boiling point of an angry outburst. Understanding your child's personality means you can lessen the impact of those trigger points. For example, do they throw tantrums when shopping at the store? Perhaps you can organize a helper when shopping, or take a favorite toy with you to keep them occupied.

❖ **Stay calm.** The last thing a confused and angry child needs is a shouting adult. They need someone around who is on their side, someone who will help them cope with their overwhelming emotions.

❖ **Be persistent.** If you have said they can't have something and that's the reason they're throwing a tantrum, don't give in. You will not be doing them, or yourself, any favors if you do. Children must learn to cope with life and all of its demands. Guide them away from whatever it is they're demanding. For example, if they're stomping their feet on the ground because you refused to let them watch TV, sit down and read a book together. Show them that there's always a way around problems, so they learn to think of this themselves. Help them resolve their frustrations.

- ❖ **Encourage** good behavior to shine through. Praise your child when they manage to calm down. Let them know that you're praising them because they're working hard to control their emotions.

- ❖ **Don't use punishments,** such as stopping their TV sessions. Instead, have a set routine whereby your child can go and sit in a particular chair while they calm down. A sort of time out routine for whenever this happens. Don't leave your child alone, though. They need you nearby to help them get through the emotion unscathed.

- ❖ **Don't try to reason** with a child in the middle of a tantrum. You will not be unable to get through to them until they've managed to calm down. It's not that they're ignoring you. It's more about being unable to balance reasoning when such a powerful emotion as anger sets in.

Don't be afraid to seek help for yourself. It can be a daunting task dealing with a child who experiences many outbursts. Parents are not trained in the skill of parenthood. It's a "learn as you go" type of job. A parent must make decisions as they go along, and they will not always get them right. Sadly, not all children have good role models in their parents. Their angry outbursts at school could be a mimicking of behavior they've witnessed at home.

There is also the possibility of a medical issue which may be exacerbating the problem. We brushed upon possible mental health problems earlier in this chapter. It's important to address such difficulties as soon as they're recognized. It can become much more difficult to resolve if such behavior continues into their teenage years. The underlying problems could have been there for years, such as bipolar disorder. Untreated, this could lead to anti-social behavior as the uncontrolled conduct escalates.

If your child is repeatedly showing uncontrollable signs of anger and you feel unable to help them, it's time to seek professional help. There's no shame in asking for help. It means that the quality of your child's life can improve. Underlying conditions, such as dyslexia or autism, can make the issues more problematic. It's far better to have a diagnosis at a young age so they can enter adulthood with an understanding of their own condition.

Dealing with Angry Teenagers

A teenager's body is in a constant state of flux most of the time. This can be due to changes to the brain and hormone imbalance. At this age, we often feel almost in a state of alienation from society, as we battle to find our identity. Hormonal changes can begin as early as 7 years of age.

As well as causing acne and hair growth on their bodies, such changes can also lead to wild mood swings. For the youngster whose life has been hindered with bad experiences as well, this is almost certainly going to lead to low esteem levels. Such youngsters will be prone to depression and anger outbursts.

As with adults, the best way to overcome these personal anger problems is with lots of support. Those with a stable family background will most likely scrape through their teenage years unharmed. They will come through as healthy well-balanced grown-ups. Whilst those from broken families may develop mental health issues that can turn them into problematic adults. These are the youngsters who need the most guidance to get through into adulthood with some degree of normality. Such teenagers probably make-up the majority of all angry adults.

Most children will act out certain characteristic traits based on what they've witnessed in their role models. Usually, this is the parents or primary caregivers. It's important as a parent to be aware of this and set a good example. Don't show too much aggression yourself in the home; it really isn't good for the children.

As a parent, if you can reflect on your own teenage years, you will remember how influential your peer groups were. These are important years for forming friendships. At the same time, it's also a time to develop their own incivility. The parents have a lot on their hands and will need to have much in the way of "patience."

Typical teenage behavior can involve eating everything in the refrigerator or being rude to family members, plus many more antisocial tendencies. Loss of temper may result in the banging of doors and disobedience of family rules. To be fair to these mini-adults, they have a lot to contend with:

- ❖ Grueling study and sitting exams can cause terrible worry.
- ❖ Embarking on romantic relationships and finding their niche within their peer group.

They have not yet developed the maturity to deal with these often emotionally-taxing problems. The problems pound at them on a daily basis with seemingly no rest period. No longer do they see their parents as their confidante. In fact, it's often a time of rebellion against their parents and their values.

Parents must be willing to negotiate and compromise. The teenagers will not be looking to compromise on their new-found vivacity for life and independence. Instead, they will expect everything to go their way. Whatever rules you lay down as a parent of teenagers, always leave a way out for them. Don't back them into corners, because they will bite. They are still your children and deserve your love and admiration for the things they do manage to achieve, such as getting out of bed on a morning. It is true that teenagers need more sleep than at any other age.

These are only the rules for a well-balanced family. For teenagers who come from families where their parents can't wait for them to leave home, there lays an even bigger problem. If you are a teenager with unhappy family relationships, seek the help of other adults in your life. Look to teachers, or even visit your doctor to get help with any depression that might be building up. Keep yourself occupied and learn as much as you can. Knowledge will help you move on once you're old enough and become independent.

Dealing with angry teenagers is as difficult as dealing with an angry adult. It should be dealt with in the same way. Angry people need help if their anger is uncontrollable. They don't need pity; they need a guiding hand and small push in the right direction.

Chapter 4

DIFFERENT TYPES OF ANGER

Painful Emotions

It's important to have an understanding of what causes an angry outburst in the first place. There are different types of frustrations and rage, and they can build up in our minds until we're fit to burst. How we deal with them depends on our own personality and upbringing.

Anger is emotional pain; that's why it comes under the heading of mental health. The health of our mind is key to resolving the symptoms you might feel in an angry flair-up.

Stages of an Angry Outburst

Let's have a look at how a flair-up might play out.

- ❖ Initially, you might feel angry through frustration, rejection, loss, or annoyance. This will be targeted at someone or something that has happened. These are negative emotions that we can all feel inside.

- ❖ Once psyched up, the hormones begin to play their part. That's when some of us start to lose control. Sometimes that pain is then directed at someone else. Or, we direct it at ourselves and cause even more mental health harm.
- ❖ When the anger is in full swing, it overrides the painful emotion that triggered it. Now, we almost feel as if we will burst out to find a sense of release to the build-up of anger.
- ❖ As the anger builds, so too the sense of power and self-defense. This is when you could start to direct negative words at the target of your anger. That aggressiveness can then lead on to being confrontational and violent.
- ❖ There is a strong sense to seek revenge, or punishment, or to hurt those who instigated the pain in the first place.

Anger Threshold

Every one of us has a different anger threshold and different ways of projecting our anger. Often this can be:

❖ Withdrawing

Looking calm on the outside but withdrawing inside yourself while the feeling passes. Withholding your emotions can be harmful because you have no outlet. It may take a long time before you feel calm again.

❖ Becoming Loud

This could manifest as shouting abusive words and becoming argumentative or feeling a need to lash out at everyone and everything.

❖ Always angry

Life is one big struggle because everyone is against you. The system is against you, and no one ever wants to help. On the contrary, they only want what is yours. Some call a person with this type of anger as someone who has a "chip on their shoulder."

❖ In Denial

Such people don't or won't admit that they have become angry. Nothing is ever resolved because there is no problem in the first place.

Research suggests that on average, each person gets angry at least once a day. Yet they may experience a small annoyance at least three times a day. If the annoyances are well managed, then your body will not suffer from the annoyance turning into anger.

Another problem with showing your anger is that it can have a domino effect. Those around you may get angry back at you. That's because anger is a natural part of self-preservation. It becomes a problem when a person uses it as their everyday way to express themselves. Such people are not only angry with themselves but with everyone who passes through their lives. They struggle to fit into their social surroundings, such as holding a job down or even having a relationship.

Six Dimensions of Anger

A study conducted in 2008 argued that there are six dimensions to how anger can be directed.

1. Reflective or Deflective

Reflected anger is generally in response to some source of provocation. It is retaliatory in nature. This type of anger can run out of control as each player increases their retaliatory action.

Deflection is completely different. This doesn't even need any provocation. Often, the victims are innocent of any wrongdoing. They become the target as the angry person instinctively shifts the blame. The aggressor cannot see how they themselves have done anything wrong. Indeed, they see themselves as the victim.

2. Internal or external

Not all anger is directed at a third party.

Internal anger is withheld and controlled, so others cannot see it. The angry person may be seething within but doesn't wish to reveal their true feelings. They may even feel the need to spare someone the hurtfulness that an angry outburst can cause. Other reasons for internalized anger can have more sinister motives. It's held in check until the perfect moment arrives to exact revenge. Then, it's released with precise planning, so there are no repercussions to the aggressor.

External anger is the process of projecting your anger on others, most often in response to offensive stimuli. The stronger the anger, the more likely the aggressor is to present it in an external fashion. Externalized anger can show itself in various ways, from facial expressions to verbal utterances or sometimes even in the physical form of aggressive mannerisms.

3. Resist or Retaliate

When confronted with a situation that invokes anger, we have two options of dealing with it.

One option is to resist anger. This doesn't mean the aggressor does nothing, but they won't show an outward display of aggression. Instead, they may become non-communicative or even defiant. They could convey a sense of detachment from the person who caused their wrath.

Retaliation can result from the trading of insults. This can progress to the exchange of physical blows. It's what's termed in international relations as "Open warfare." This type of response can soon get out of hand and often result in injury.

4. Physical or Verbal Expression

Generally, when we experience anger, our outlet can take one of two forms. These are verbal or non-verbal.

With nonverbal expression, it's not only what we say, but how we say it. Studies on vocal acoustics in angry people show that for many, their voice raises to a higher pitched level. It will be loud in volume, with the use of a fast tempo. Often, it may become littered with abusive words and expletives. Although that's not always the case, some can appear calm. This type of person will be quietly spoken but heap sarcasm onto their target.

Nonverbal or physical communications of anger may not involve violence. It will become most obvious in the facial area. This can be combined with other body postures and gesticulations, such as hand movement and gait. Sometimes, this behavior can lead to more aggressive actions, such as striking, kicking, or pushing.

5. Uncontrolled or Controlled

Controlling anger has interested psychologists and philosophers throughout the ages. To be able to take control of your own anger requires a good deal of thoughtfulness. This will also include a modification of behavior. In essence, it is a reflective process rather than a reflexive one. It's important to understand that controlling anger does not mean it is eliminated. Rather, it is a process of management.

Uncontrolled anger can, in fact, be a psychological problem. It is a topic included in the psychologist's bible, The Diagnostic and Statistical Manual of Mental Disorders, (DSM).

When an angry response is so much out of proportion to the trigger, it is known as Intermittent Explosive Disorder. This uncontrolled display of anger is not always a physical response but can also be vocal in nature.

6. Punitive or Restorative

Our trigger to anger may depend on whether the perpetrator feels any remorse at stirring up our emotions. This is restorative anger, whereby an apology or regret may help to calm us down. It can depend on the severity of the offense that caused the anger, though. Generally, the desire to move on and get over it all is the main motive of restorative anger.

At the other end of the scale is punitive anger. This is where retribution is the driving force. No apology or offer of recompense can salve the anger of the injured party. Their behavior can become almost obsessive in not being willing to forgive or forget. The type of character who cannot accept this will be unable to move on. They may hold a grudge and look to find a means of getting even with the individual who caused their anger.

Intermittent Explosive Disorder IED

We have brushed upon this earlier in the guide, but IED is an impulse control condition. It can result in an aggressive outburst that is out of proportion to the provocation. This is a volatile type of anger and can happen for no clear reason. Following the explosive outburst, the sufferer will feel a great sense of relief. Later, they may also feel shame and guilt at their uncontrollable behavior.

Around 11-16 million Americans may suffer IED at some time in their lives. This is a recognized psychological disorder. Although there has been no gene identified with the behavior, it is believed to pass from parent to child. A child's environment plays a crucial part in their behavioral development. When raised to receive hard physical punishments, some may replicate such behavior as adults. It can show its ugly head when they lose their temper. There is a range of symptoms in the current iteration of DSM.

Research indicates it may be a cause of abnormalities in certain areas of the brain. Scientists believe IED to be linked to the neurotransmitter known as serotonin. Also to the production of the hormone testosterone. These dysfunctional regions include the limbic system. If you recall, this is part of the brain that deals with emotions and memories. It is situated at the prefrontal lobe of the brain, that regulates impulses among other processes.

People with IED are more likely to abuse others. They find themselves involved in social angry situations, such as road rage. This is because they have a low tolerance range. It's a form of emotional detachment in that they have tunnel vision for those few small moments. Sufferers will experience the physical symptoms of their rage. They can suffer any of the typical reactions to stress. This can include palpitations, tightening of the chest, or headache from raised blood pressure.

It is a disorder that can lead to an abusive adult being unable to experience any positive relationships.

Typically, they may even abuse their own children, and so the cycle continues.

IED can take hold of a person in other situations too:

- ❖ Anyone who experiences trauma and suffers Post-Traumatic Stress Disorder (PTSD).
- ❖ Those with Attention Deficit Hyperactivity Disorder (ADHD) can be gripped with IED.
- ❖ Individuals who have Bi-polar Disorder can go on to develop IED.

The good side of this condition is that it has been identified as a mental health issue and as such, can be diagnosed and treated. With the right professional help, the sufferer can learn certain management disciplines. These will assist in controlling their angry flare-ups. People who suffer extreme anger outbursts are not necessarily bad people. They are mostly people who have suffered bad experiences, which have affected their personal growth.

Treatments can include:

- ❖ Medication

- Individual therapy
- Group therapy
- Family therapy
- Recreational programs
- Rehabilitation admittance, in the form of a Partial Hospitalization Program (PHP)
- Outpatient Appointments include an intensive period of therapy by visiting a clinic for sessions.

Chapter 5

IS ANGER THE SAME FOR MEN AND WOMEN?

Neural Wiring in Men and Women

Research at Southwest Missouri State University (SMSU), in 2010, found differences in anger control between the genders

- ❖ Men felt constricted if they had to hold their anger inside and could not express it whereas women were more comfortable putting anger on hold.
- ❖ Women see anger as a way to release their frustrations, rather than an aggressive outburst. For this reason, they will seek answers to the cause. Such as, if they constantly feel "frustrated" in their marriage, they may seek divorce.

These differences are most likely caused by pressures of expected social behavior of the genders. whereas, it's acceptable for men to show their anger but not for women. Instead, women have learned to re-direct such feelings. The research indicates that women see anger as counter-productive and so direct the emotion elsewhere.

This does not mean that women never get angry because they do. We must take into account all the other evidence we have discussed, such as upbringing and personality development. The research also found that women who hold back angry feelings are more prone to other mental health symptoms. These can include things like depression and anxiety.

Research at Monash University, in 2016, has shown that men do indeed act differently to women when in stressful situations. They tend to rely on a more hostile approach, such as fight or flight. Whereas women have a less aggressive overture towards confrontations. The researchers termed it as, "Tend and Befriend." The team who conducted the study believe this differing attitude is due to the Sex-Determining Region of Y-chromosomes, (SRY) gene. This is a DNA protein that determines our sexual gender.

However, it's not only genes that are responsible for the different ways men and women respond to anger or stress. We also need to look at the brain's physiology and the release of various hormones.

The female brain is 8% smaller than the male brain. Yet women have much better managing strategies than men. Researchers believe this is due to the variations of neural wiring in men and women's brains. The brain has two halves, referred to as hemispheres. For men, the neural wiring is front to back, with little crossing over the two hemispheres. Women have more of a crisscross pattern of neural wiring, that crosses the two hemispheres.

In conclusion, male anger can be explosive whilst for females, it comes to a simmer.

The University of Pennsylvania, School of Medicine, studied effects on the brain, when angry. They showed evidence that the brain acts differently in men and women when it comes to the raw emotion of anger. This was measured by comparing the frontal cortex area of the brain. Most women had larger areas of the Orbital Frontal Cortex (OFC) than men. Their theory is that the larger this area is, the more capable the person will be of taking control of anger. Their logic "kicks-in" quicker, and they will try to diffuse an angry situation.

It's not that women don't feel the emotion of anger, because they do. The difference is they can manage to internalize such thoughts. The result of this can be that their anger leads to stress. That sets off a whole new set of challenges to the health of the sufferer. Again, it is an emotion that triggers hormonal release. If experienced for long periods of time, stress can become a mental health illness in itself.

This study did confirm one other interesting outcome. The differences between men and women are not necessarily just based on social influences. We are a product of our genetic makeup, and that isn't something that we can control.

Scientists have measured other areas of the male and female brains, and the differences continue to show up. It does make you wonder if the sexes are in fact, different species. It brings to mind the book by John Gray, "Men Are from Mars, Women Are from Venus."

Hormonal Differences in Men and Women

The Effects of Testosterone

Testosterone is a hormone that is part of the androgen group. These are chemicals produced in the male testes and in a woman's ovary. Both males and females have androgens, but for women, they are at a much lower level. The major androgen in males is testosterone. This can make a man feel more alert both sexually and physically.

- Low testosterone levels in men not only decrease their libido but can lead to depression. They will become more irritable and lethargic.
- One study indicated that when a woman or child cries, it can reduce testosterone levels in men. A further study by Cambridge University showed that high testosterone levels reduce empathy. The study also indicated the higher the testosterone levels, the more self-centered the person becomes.
- When two people bond in positive affection, their oxytocin hormone levels rise, and testosterone levels drop although sexual activity will increase testosterone levels.
- Dangerous situations can raise testosterone levels.
- Gambling can make testosterone levels rise when on a winning streak. It gives a sense of confidence and power. Done too often and tolerance levels will become affected, so the person increases the activity. If they continue to succeed, it will give a spike of testosterone levels once again. Now the person is hooked and

constantly attempting to gain that feeling of confidence and power.

- ❖ In overweight men, excess fat tissues will increase their estrogen hormone. As a result, it lowers testosterone levels and decreases their sex drive.
- ❖ If you are a father, your testosterone levels will become around 33% lower than before you became a parent. Plus, you will likely have around 25% more oxytocin, the hormone that helps with bonding.
- ❖ One interesting fact about oxytocin is that dogs have it too. When their humans show them affection, their oxytocin levels rise.

Whilst it's true to say that men release around eight times more testosterone than women, it's not the reason why men get angrier. There have been links to a decrease in testosterone levels when men become angry.

The Effects of Estrogen

Anger in women often takes on a different form but not always of a less aggressive nature. Women may use the power of words more when angry. They may spread malicious rumors as they try to find a route to vent the negative emotion of anger. Of course, men can also use the sharp edge of their tongue when angry.

In opposition to testosterone for men, there is estrogen for women. It's produced in the ovaries. Estrogen can also be reproduced by both men and women as fat tissue if overweight.

- ❖ Low levels of estrogen for women can lead to mood swings.
- ❖ Estrogen is low during menstruation and also throughout menopause. These are typically the times when a woman becomes more irritable and is less able to cope with life's ups and downs.
- ❖ A diet of estrogen rich foods, such as flaxseed, nuts, and even red wine, is a natural way to increase this hormone.
- ❖ High levels of estrogen have been connected to breast cancer.

Hormones play a great part in our moods and behavior. These are not the only cause that can lead to mood swings and out of control emotions.

Social Differences in Men and Women

We know that the brain functions differently between the genders. Here are some other differences between the genders that support the fact that males are more aggressive than females:

- ❖ The more obvious differences are in physical appearance. Men are usually taller with broader shoulders. Women often have wider hips and larger breasts for childbirth. Men grow facial hair, and women usually have quite a smooth face with little hair growth. We share the same amount of limbs, and our internal organs are similar, though our bone structure does differ slightly.
- ❖ There is another difference that's not so evident, that of chromosomes. We share 22 of

these that are the same, with another 2 that are different according to gender.

❖ Historically, women have always been seen as the weaker sex, not only in physical strength but also in mental capacity. Of course, we now know that women can be just as intelligent as men, yet society still treats them as the weaker sex. Gender inequality is often at the top of many politicians' agenda. Perhaps one day in the future, all people regardless of their gender or ethnicity will be treated as equals, but we're not there yet.

❖ In one survey, 54% of men believed gender differences were biological. Yet 67% of women believed that it's more of a social problem.

❖ Whilst the workforce is evenly split, men are still considered the main breadwinner. Though this is changing with at least 40% of women becoming the primary breadwinner in their family.

Men tend to be the risk takers, whereas most women tend to be cautious. This could be why statistics show that men are more likely to die from an accident than women.

One researcher at the University of California believes that "The female brain has evolved to avoid physical outbursts. This means that their children are less likely to get hurt."

Does this all fall back to our ancestral behavior when men would hunt and protect, and women banded together to make a home and keep the children safe?

If men were unable to vent their aggression in a physical manner, would they be more likely to evolve with similarities to the female biology of the brain?

One thing is for sure. There are clear biological differences, and these have most likely led to social differences.

Chapter 6

Identifying Anger Issues

One symptom often seen in someone who loses their control regularly is that they are usually the last person to realize what they've done. That's because they are often in denial and afraid to admit to any such weakness.

To cure this character flaw, they must first be able to admit that they have a problem. As with addiction, it is a mental health issue that can be rectified with help. Though if you cannot admit that you have a problem, then how can you cure it if it doesn't exist in your mind? You have to be ready to make changes in your life.

Broken relationships are often a common problem for those with anger issues, more so if their anger outbursts result in violence.

We know that anger is an emotion, and as such, we can all feel it on the odd occasion. There may be times when we can feel more irritable than normal:

- ❖ A woman's menstrual cycle results in unbalanced hormones. This can result in many emotional symptoms, including feeling more irritable.
- ❖ Men tend to bottle up their emotions more often than not. This can have a similar effect as a ticking bomb or a pressure cooker. It can explode at any moment.

It's important to understand the symptoms of an anger disorder, so you are aware of the risks. Learn to know your own signs that your emotions are negative.

How often do you feel:

- ❖ Irritable
- ❖ Anxious
- ❖ Stressed
- ❖ Annoyed with just about everyone

These are normal emotions to feel on the odd occasion. If you're feeling them on a daily basis, the chances are you'll also lose your temper more often.

Self-Harming

Anger can show its ugly face in many forms. One such form can be self-harming.

- ❖ A person who feels the need to harm themselves is experiencing unsafe thought patterns.
- ❖ They are most likely already suffering from an array of negative emotions, such as anxiety and stress.
- ❖ They tend to blame themselves for every mishap they go through. As they pent up their emotions, there is no outlet. This leads to a feeling of losing control. At this point, they may self-harm to take back some control of their life.
- ❖ It could be that they feel their anger is out of control. By injuring themselves, it will give them focus elsewhere, so the anger subsides.
- ❖ Or, it could be that instead of hitting out at others, they harm themselves.

- In a sense, they don't wish to burden others. If someone does attempt to help them, they will feel even more guilty at imposing their problems upon them.
- Whilst self-harming makes them feel more in control, the truth is that they are losing control.
- They have no coping strategies in place. This makes them feel completely overwhelmed, resulting in negative emotions.
- Self-harming may be their own form of punishment.
- Or, as anger sets in, they may self-harm on impulse.
- Afterward, they may hide the injury through a feeling of shame.
- Or, they may seek attention for the injury. By showing someone their pain, they can now accept outside help because there is a plausible reason to do so.

One thing many self-harmers have in common is a self-loathing of themselves, at least at the time, they are harming. This is a common form of expression in the teenage years. Once again, hormonal imbalance is ruling behavior. The body is going through changes from being a child to becoming an adolescent. Sadly, it can go on into adulthood. In general, though, teenagers do learn other ways of coping as they mature and will stop self-harming.

Other forms that anger can present itself might be:

- A lack of patience for others.
- Speaking rudely to people, often without any real reason.
- Blaming other people for everything that is wrong in your life.
- Being sarcastic at another person's expense.
- Threatening other people.
- Raising your voice most of the time.
- Clenching your jaws often.
- Sweaty palms or sticky neckline.
- A feeling that you need to explode, such as shouting and lashing out in an aggressive manner.

If you think these are familiar feelings and you experience them on a daily basis, then it's time to take responsibility and seek help, not only help for yourself but for those around you and your loved ones. You may not realize that you've been taking out your anger on them because you may well be in deep denial.

You're making yourself mentally and physically ill. Those closest to you will also be feeling similar feelings as they see you suffer. They themselves are subject to your wild outbursts of anger.

Road Rage

What is it that can make calm people into monsters when they get behind the wheel of a vehicle? It's such a strange phenomenon!

Passengers in the vehicle don't particularly serve as a buffer. The driver may still rage at other drivers on the road, even with their children present.

Whilst road rage may seem to be a minor problem as we can all lose our tempers when witnessing bad driving, it can have serious consequences.

Road rage is an incident whereby a driver becomes verbally or physically abusive to another driver or pedestrian. Sometimes, it can lead to dangerous driving as they use their vehicle in an aggressive manner. Drivers who act with uncontrollable rage could be suffering from Intermittent Explosive Disorder (IED). The American Automobile Association's studies show that men are the main culprits. They caused 96% of road rage incidents in the past and averaged around the age of 33-years old.

Road rage was a factor in over 400 fatalities on the roads in the USA in 2015. This might seem a low figure, but it is a growing problem. The National Highway Traffic Safety Administration informs us this problem has increased by nearly 500% in the last ten years.

The risk from road rage is not always the fault of other drivers. If you act in this way, it could be you that hurts yourself and your passengers. The loss of anger control will inevitably lead to dangerous driving. Even if it doesn't lead to an accident, your loss of temper is bad for your heart. Your blood pressure will increase, which is a major factor of cardiovascular disease.

Where does a driver's patience go? Is it:

- A need for control?
- A violation of our personal space, which is a much larger area when we're sitting in a car.
- Primitive hormones?
- Lack of intellect?

One thing is for sure; it's a risky business and could easily lead to:

- Accidents
- Arrests and fines
- Assaults
- Families falling out with each other
- Embarrassment
- Lawsuits

With the intense release of hormones comes an increase in stress levels. That's what's happening to make drivers so angry with each other. It doesn't need to be a long journey because it boils down to a lack of compassion and control. Control your angry thoughts and stop blaming everyone else. It doesn't matter who's to blame so long as no one is hurt. Only then will the release of hormones slow down and stop your angry explosion.

One of the major problems is that most drivers expect other drivers to behave as they do. This leads to them feeling offended if someone else's driving habits clash with their own.

Such easily-offended drivers will be busy thinking:

- ❖ Why won't they leave the junction quicker? They're holding everyone up.
- ❖ Why are they driving so slow?
- ❖ How dare they tailgate me?
- ❖ I'm going to make sure I get off first when the traffic signals change color!
- ❖ The cheek of it, they're trying to overtake me. I'm going to speed up!

If you're a regular driver, then these statements may sound familiar to you.

We're all meant to wait for our turn in a fair system. Yet, when traffic's moving slow, we tend to think we're the only ones who are stuck. Or, we are the only ones who are in a rush. Guess what? Everyone has somewhere they need to be; that's why they're on their journey in the first place.

For many, manners can disappear when someone aggravates them. Down goes the window and they shout out at who has offended them, or they make obscene gestures. In reality, all it achieves is making the situation worse.

This is a form of anger that can get most of us hot under the collar, and it isn't good for anyone; victim or perpetrator.

It's so easy to say that the next time it happens, we will deal with it better. The trouble is, our emotions are on overdrive, pun intended.

Here are a few suggestions on how to keep yourself calm whilst sitting in your vehicle:

- ❖ Don't forget the breathing techniques. Should you feel that anger stirring in the pit of your stomach over some annoyance whilst driving, take that deep breath through your nose. Follow it through as in the relaxation breathing exercises.
- ❖ It helps if you don't play fast music on the radio while you drive, this can feed your aggression. Instead, play something a little more soothing so you keep your calm should someone annoy you on your journey.
- ❖ Listen to a podcast, though without earphones on so you can still hear the traffic. This forces your thoughts elsewhere as you listen to the person speaking. Of course, your full concentration needs to be on the road, so it should only be background noise.
- ❖ Stop traveling everywhere as if you're in a hurry. If you are, then set off earlier and don't get so stressed if traffic holds you up. Good

planning should mean you have less urgency. When calculating your timing, you should allow for hiccups along the way. If there are none, then you'll get there earlier.

❖ Don't drive when you're tired. Your mind is foggy, so you're unable to give you full attention to the skill of driving. There are many fatal accidents on the roads caused by drivers falling asleep at the wheel.

❖ If something does happen and you're approached by another driver, swallow your pride and show them a warm smile. Even if it's not your fault, apologize anyway so long as there's no harm done. It takes far more guts to apologize than it does to argue back.

Use all those new skills you are practicing, such as empathy, compromising, and forgiveness. Yes, there are many bad drivers out there, but as a driver, you already know that. If you don't like it, then don't drive. Otherwise, you must learn to put up with the incompetence of other people. If someone's tailgating you, let them past. They clearly haven't read any guides to teach them how to be a calmer individual. They may not be very nice people in the first place, so don't risk harm to yourself, your passengers, or your vehicle.

Even if the other driver has broken the law, don't confront them. If you have a dashcam, then you could go to the police later.

Most of the time, road rage is over nothing much to start with. In many instances, the drivers will have an altercation and then continue on their way. They will still experience the negative vibes of the situation. This, in itself, may cause them to suffer the consequences of the incident for hours afterward. Far better to brush the incident off and accept it's all "par for the course." Sooner or later, you're going to come across a bad driver, accept this as a fact of life.

We all expect people to abide by the rules in our society. Yet, when on the road, reckless drivers disrupt this very system outright. They do things that are unfair and unjust, and we all want to punish them for it. It is far better to ignore such deviant folks and hope they get their comeuppance over their ignorant driving skills.

Sooner or later, they'll do something wrong which might be seen by the police. It's inevitable for such people who drive without care or respect.

Where to get help for Anger Management

One way to find help for your anger issues is to search out any local support groups for anger management. You can do this by enquiring with:

- ❖ A doctor.
- ❖ A chemist in your area.
- ❖ Any health clinic.
- ❖ Online research.

At these groups, you will meet fellow sufferers, people who are going through the same experiences as you. There is no easy solution, and in some ways, it is willpower that will get you through. It will be easier with others helping you through the difficult process. Once you manage to learn how to control your anger, you will become a much happier person, and your family will be happier too.

There's a variety of medications that can help tremendously. Your doctor will need to know about your anger flare-ups and any depression that often goes hand-in-hand with anger.

Admit to yourself that you have a mental health problem. It is not a label, but an illness that's caused by an imbalance in your brain and hormones. That's why medication works so well. Once your hormones are stable, you can then learn coping strategies. By taking such action, you know that you're well on your way to being a better person, not that an angry person is a bad person unless they're hurting others intentionally. It will be worth it as you begin to feel healthier along with your new lifestyle.

Chapter 7

LIFESTYLE CHANGES

You might be thinking that making lifestyle changes is something that someone else would do, not you. Or, that it's something people do when they're recovering from an illness. On top of those thoughts, you most likely believe it's all about money; commercial enterprises are trying to get you to buy their expensive "natural foods" and the latest keep-fit equipment. The truth is that it's none of those scenarios. What it really means is ridding your life of bad habits. It does not need to cost money, but if you don't improve your lifestyle, it will cost you your health.

Dietary Needs

Let's start right at the very basics with the food that you put into your body. What's this got to do with anger management, you ask? You're quite right; this isn't a dietary book. Yet, there is a need to understand how the human body works if you are to make positive changes in your life.

The natural processes that take place in your digestive system are a result of the types of food you choose to put in there. If you eat unhealthily, such as choosing high carbohydrate foods, then your body will suffer the consequences. Such foods are poisonous to the body, and here's why:

- ❖ The gut absorbs foods for nutrients. Healthy foods, such as vegetables and whole-wheat ingredients, break down at a slow rate. This means your body benefits from the rich nutrients. It then passes through into the small intestine. From there, the nutrients enter the bloodstream. Next, they're directed to the pancreas and liver to use up the glucose, vitamins, and proteins.
- ❖ Some foods pass into the bloodstream much quicker, such as carbohydrates. By entering quicker, they don't get broken down and turn into glucose. Too much glucose results in a

spike in blood sugars. The food that has caused a sugar spike then triggers the pancreas to produce insulin. Too much insulin can lead to becoming insulin resistant, known as diabetes type 2.

- ❖ When we have an excess supply of glucose, the body doesn't need it all. Rather than waste it, it is turned into fat and stored away in case we need extra energy at some point. Hence, we now start to put on weight.

This is a simple analogy of how harmful eating high carb foods can be for your body. It's not only diabetes type 2 that can be a consequence of eating unhealthy foods. There are a whole host of bad conditions that come from having too much fat in storage.

- ❖ Being unable to sleep
- ❖ High blood pressure
- ❖ Heart diseases
- ❖ Strokes
- ❖ Certain cancers
- ❖ Liver diseases

- ❖ Kidney diseases
- ❖ Unhealthy bones leading to osteoarthritis

It's a long and worrying list, but it is also an avoidable list of conditions.

Exercise

That dreaded word!

Before you let out a sigh of, "here we go again," bear in mind that we're discussing your health.

We're not talking about jogging for miles until you drop, or even paying extortionate gym fees. It's simply a case of stopping yourself from becoming too sedentary. Exercising regularly can help a lot in regards to keeping your mind clear.

Let's first discuss what happens to your body when you exercise, even just a little. Whether suffering anger issues or not, we should all exercise as recommended by the health authorities.

Avoid Inactivity at all costs!!

Every week, you should do the minimum of medium-intensity exercise for at least 2 hours and 30 minutes throughout the whole week.

That means you can split it into:

- ❖ 5-days x 30-minute sessions.
- ❖ Or, 5 days at 15 minutes on a morning, and 15 minutes during the afternoon.

There is no need for a rigid and painful exercise routine. Depending on your age and circumstances, a brisk walk could fulfill the criteria.

This is not enough exercise to lose weight, but it's enough to keep your heart fairly healthy.

That's why there is a little more besides the medium level of exercise. Don't worry. It only amounts to an extra 1 hour and 15 minutes a week doing a more vigorous exercise regime. You may know this type of exercise as aerobics. It means the exercise should be designed to make your heart pump a little faster, resulting in making you short of breath. Here are a few ideas on how you can achieve this part:

- ❖ Add another 15 minutes to the walks you do already as outlined above, only walk faster, or uphill.
- ❖ 2 x 35-minute swimming sessions a week.
- ❖ 3 x 25-minute sessions of cycling.
- ❖ Get a home rowing machine and row for 15 minutes x 5 days.
- ❖ Start dancing lessons.

In total, it means you should be exercising for around 4 hours in the entire week. That's not a lot of your time!

Sleep

By making simple changes in your lifestyle, such as eating healthy foods and doing the minimal of exercise, your body will start to feel better. This, in turn, will lead to better sleep, and that in itself will help reduce the feelings of irritability.

How much sleep is enough?

It is not a myth; teenagers really do need more sleep. As we enter our teen years, we should be getting around 8-

10 hours of sleep. From around 18 years onwards, between 7-9 hours should suffice, depending on your metabolism.

If you don't get the right type and amount of sleep, you will:

- ❖ Be less able to concentrate throughout your waking hours.
- ❖ Have a slower and more ineffective immunity system. This results in catching those annoying bugs and viruses that spread around rapidly and will not help with your mood.
- ❖ Increasing the chances of heart disease, as your heart rate is affected if you don't get enough sleep,
- ❖ Whilst too little sleep is harmful, so too is having too much sleep. A study by researchers at Keele University indicates that those who sleep longer than 8 hours have an increased risk of heart attack and premature death.
- ❖ Inadequate sleep results in mood swings, which can lead to accidents if you're feeling

argumentative. If this happens on a regular basis, it can ruin your quality of life.

American Academy of Sleep Medicine (AASM) informs us that only 1 in 3 adults is getting adequate sleep. That leaves a lot of tired and irritable adults walking around; let's hope you're not one of them.

Remember this easy equation: a healthy diet plus the recommended amount of exercise will equal a good night's sleep. If you feel more refreshed when you wake up, then your mind will be clearer to face the ups and downs of the day ahead. Now that you can concentrate better, you can begin to teach yourself to have more positive thoughts. Push away those negative ones; you don't need them in your life.

This is not an easy thing to do when under stress, or you've had bad experiences in your life. None of these changes are going to be easy, but they are all necessary if you want to bring your anger under control. To be successful in this, you need the right mindset and thinking patterns. That's why it's so critical to get yourself on track with the right diet, exercise, and sleep.

What then is a positive mindset?

First and foremost, it is about changing your own mental attitude and not about making those around you change.

People who display symptoms of aggressive, angry bouts are the most likely to allow their negative thoughts to rule their heads. It can be made worse because of depression or stress. Often it festers because of a bad experience or a difficult relationship. There can be any number of valid reasons that have unbalanced their lives. When the mind is so confused that it causes stress, it's a time to call for help. Self-help is a good way to start. The responsibility lies within ourselves to make these changes in our lives. If you can help yourself, it opens the way for other people to help you too.

We must learn to push away our negative thoughts and replace them with more positive thinking patterns. This will also involve using and altering our communication skills. If we can communicate better with others, we can learn to understand their point of view. It is a start to learning to use the skill of empathy.

There is a difference between empathy and sympathy, the latter being that you feel sorry, or even pity, someone else. Empathy is not pity. It is being able to put yourself in someone's place and understand how they feel.

Let's look at an example of this.

- ❖ You see someone on the street asking for money.
- ❖ Your first thought could be that they want money for drugs or alcohol. Negative thinking! Then again, you don't want to be naive and ignore such truths.
- ❖ Your second thought could be that they are lazy and should get a job. Negative thinking! You know nothing of how or why they are in the situation they are living. Don't be so judgmental!

Ask yourself why anyone would live that way voluntarily? If you can do this, it means that you're starting to see their situation from their point of view.

Consider a few reasons why they might be in that situation, such as:

- ❖ Are they recently divorced and ended up homeless?
- ❖ If it's a teenager, then it could be that their parents don't care about them. They may not even have any parents to guide them?
- ❖ If it's a woman, she could have been in a violent relationship and ran away from her home to get away from it.

There could be so many reasons why this person finds themselves in the situation they're in.

No one is saying that you have to give them money. It could be that are dependent on drugs or alcohol. It's not unusual for those in such difficult circumstances to follow such a path. If you want to help them, then consider buying them a sandwich or an item of warm clothing. Or simply talk to them, it might be just what they need to feel human again.

The main thing is not to have negative thoughts about others you know nothing about.

The positive way to think is:

- ❖ Not to be judgmental of others.
- ❖ Try to be more empathic of what other people are thinking and experiencing as they too go about their daily toil.
- ❖ Help other people when you can.
- ❖ Don't hold grudges when someone does something wrong to you. All this does is eat away at you, making you feel negative those emotions. Learn to let the grudge go.
- ❖ Be as forgiving as possible. It's not easy, but realize that people do make mistakes. If their errors have an impact on your life, the chances are it was not intentional. Even if it was, learn to rise above pettiness and move on.
- ❖ Behave in an ethical way. Make an attempt to understand others and the reasons they make mistakes. We return to empathy later because it is such an important skill to learn. You must

find the strength to take on some of these challenges. They are not easy by any means. We are all challenged in this world to make the best of our situations.

The next time you feel anger welling up inside, ask yourself questions. Why is that person behaving the way they are? Try to understand the argument or situation from their point of view. Most of all, learn how to ignore the people that you cannot learn to like. It's okay not to like certain people, but learn to shut them out of your own life. If they cross your pathway, let them go by freely. With a positive mindset, you can learn to cope with many difficult people and situations.

In the next chapter, we will look at techniques for helping you to take control of your anger impulses.

Chapter 8

Anger Management Techniques & Exercises

If you suffer from uncontrollable anger bouts, then you will benefit by learning certain control techniques. Instead of swimming the moat around and around your castle, open up the castle doors and let the help flow in.

Help from Others

One thing you must learn to do is accept help from other people when it's offered. Without others in your life, making changes can be a much more difficult task.

Medication

There are certain drugs that can be very helpful for uncontrollable mood swings. You must speak to a doctor or clinician so they can assess the right medication for your personal situation. As we explained earlier, much of our body is ruled by chemicals called hormones. The right medication can balance out the neurotransmitters in the brain, which in turn allows you to cope with your moods. Neurotransmitters are nerves and cells that are interconnected in the brain. They are triggered into action by the hormones we produce.

Therapy Sessions

You can do this privately or be referred by a doctor. It means attending sessions whereby you can talk about your personal experiences. It's a great opportunity to express your mental health concerns to a professional who can help with diagnosis. You may prefer one-to-one therapy, or go to group sessions, or both. Groups will consist of other people experiencing similar problems. It is a place to share your symptoms and worries. Therapy has proved successful for many with their mental health issues.

The best people to help with any type of mental health problems are the professionals. They are the experts in their field. After many years of studying, they will have a full understanding of the biological processes that cause such problems. Their hard gained knowledge means they know the best procedures on how to relieve relevant symptoms. Here are a few ways the experts can help you with the popular cognitive behavior therapy. Remember though; treatment results vary for each individual.

Communication skills

Angry people who become uncontrollably frustrated may feel as though no one understands their point of view. Whenever they try to put it across, they may become further annoyed as others disagree with them. Their reaction is to block others off and not listen. By improving their own communication skills, they will be better able to get their thoughts across to other people. Our instincts tell us to keep a distance from aggressive situations because they might be a threat to us. So, instead of shouting at others, the aggressor should learn how to get their opinion over in a calm manner. That is all it will take to get other people to listen.

Problem Solving

Many people who have mixed emotions prefer to shut their minds off from problems that come at them. This is a mistake, as rarely do problems resolve themselves, so they're unlikely to go away. When they come back a second time, they're usually even worse. It is far better to learn skills that will help aggressors confront problems in their lives. Sometimes, just being able to collect their thoughts will direct them to look at logical solutions. For instance, debts can be handled with the right guidance. Access to seeing children in a marital breakdown can be handled with the right mindset and professional guidance. Poverty does not mean you have to starve; there are ways of finding access to food banks. There are always solutions if you can get your mind focused on finding and accepting them.

Avoidance

Those of us who suffer low self-esteem prefer to avoid other people and situations, particularly those involving problem-solving. It's important for them to learn how to confront their inner demons. These are often in the form of memories. An aggressive person might feel brave when they're screaming, shouting, and lashing out. All that serves is to show how frustrated they are. Avoidance only puts things off temporarily, so it's vital to learn skills to help you cope.

Humor

They say a smile can make all the difference, and a laugh can turn your life around. There is rarely find anything to laugh at in therapy, but with the right treatment, you will laugh again. With the right kind of help, you will learn that there is another side to life that is not always negative. Sometimes, you can learn to appreciate nature and the world around you, once you realize it's there. Though it's more about learning to think positive thoughts and banish the negative ones. It's not only about learning how to control your anger, but also about learning how to control your emotions. Once you know how to deal with the negative ones, such as sad or disturbing memories, you will become a happier person. Humor can be a great healer.

Self Help

Once you recognize that you have a problem with your emotions, you are halfway on the road to recovery. It takes a strength of character to admit your own weaknesses. There are many who will not. If the symptoms we have discussed in this guide apply to you, then there is a way forward. Recognizing the problem is the first step.

Now you must find the strength to tackle your internal insecurities. We all have them. The best way forward is to turn your life around. For some, the symptoms may not show on the surface, but it doesn't mean they aren't struggling on the inside.

The following self-help exercises have proven to help calm stresses and dampen anger.

Breathing Exercises

This one is so easy that you can do it anywhere, anytime. People who are feeling angry will often breathe rapidly as their anger increases. If you feel this happening, then force yourself to:

- ❖ Take a deep breath through your nose and count to four. Counting in your mind also helps you to concentrate and takes your mind away from the offending incident. Hold that breath for a count of six, and then let it out as if you are pushing out all your fiery emotions.
- ❖ With the second repeat of this breathing technique, as you inhale allow your belly to expand outwards. Your chest will rise a little but try and concentrate the air into your stomach. Hold for a count of six again, and exhale through your mouth.

Repeat this as many times as you need, and the process of the exercise will be a distraction that will help to calm you down. Not only that, but you are increasing the oxygen levels in your bloodstream. This helps to lower blood pressure that would normally build-up with stress.

You can be standing, sitting, or even lying down, if possible. Learn to incorporate this relaxation exercise into your life. It's not only for when you feel you might explode with anger, but it's also a great de-stressor. If you get to take a break and sit down, this exercise will help you wind down for a few moments.

Muscle and Joint Relaxation Exercises

It's better if you can lay down for this exercise, but you can still do a smaller version of it if you're standing or sitting. It's more of a soothing relaxation method, rather than an instant fix. Let's assume something has upset you and you are feeling tense. Walk away from the situation and attempt these relaxation techniques. You'll be so busy concentrating on these exercises that you'll naturally become calmer.

The whole routine can take at least half an hour or longer. If you have time to do the full workout, it incorporates the entire body. If you only have time to perform one or two parts, count to at least ten in your mind before you move between body parts.

- ❖ Close your eyes if you can, but don't worry if you can't. The main task is to focus for a minute or two until you calm down.

- ❖ If you are doing the entire workout, then start at the far extremities of your body, your toes. Wiggle them around for a count of 5 seconds. Follow this by squeezing any muscles you can feel in your foot. We're not always aware of foot muscles because it's not something we consciously think about. Be careful not to get a cramp because we don't often give these muscles such attention.
- ❖ Move your concentration to your ankles. Circle both feet around one way, then circle them around the other way.
- ❖ Move on to your calves. Squeeze those calf muscles as hard as you can on both legs, then relax and loosen the tense muscle. Do this around 10 times.
- ❖ Next, move up to the knees. You'll need some room for this exercise, so if space is tight, give it a miss. Bend those knees and then straighten the legs out and do this to both legs 10 times.
- ❖ Now squeeze the thigh muscles underneath, then relax. Repeat at least ten times. Then repeat but squeeze the top of the thighs.

The idea is to work your way through your body. Next could be your buttock cheeks, and then maybe your stomach muscles, chest, shoulders, tops of arms, and the bottom of arms; squeeze each muscle and then relax it to the count of 10 times each.

- ❖ Rotate your shoulders and shrug them up and down. Push them backward, upwards and any which way that you can feel muscles pulling.
- ❖ When you get to the hands, spend some time stretching out your fingers and rotating your wrists around. Squeeze whatever muscles you can feel in your hands but again be careful of cramps.
- ❖ Rotate your neck in full circles one way and then the other. Tense the muscles so you can feel them pulling on your shoulders. This part is a great routine if you have a headache.
- ❖ Finish on your face and open your mouth as wide as you can, pushing your jaw downwards. Pull faces to stretch the facial muscles and the neck tendons. Squeeze your eyes open and shut many times. Do as much as you can to feel all

the different muscles in your face that you're normally aware of.
- ❖ Before you open up your eyes again, do those breathing exercises if you have time.

What this entire workout achieves is a total relaxation of all your muscles and joints. It takes some time to do a whole session, but it will leave you feeling good. When you find yourself in a stressful situation, try to sit down and do a small part of it. If you don't want anyone to notice, tense muscles they can't see, such as your thighs. The tensing and relaxing of those muscles will help you to calm down.

Visualizing

This relaxation method can give instant release to tension. It's a good way to calm a rising temper.

- ❖ Begin with a few deep breaths from the breathing exercise we discussed earlier.
- ❖ While you're focusing on your breathing regime, start to visualize a pleasant calming place. Perhaps a favorite beach, a woodland, or

anywhere else that's peaceful. Don't think about anywhere noisy, such as a football game; the idea is to get your mind into a peaceful place.

- ❖ Focus on the detail of the imaginary situation you have placed yourself in. Can you hear the sound of the ocean or the wind in the trees? What can you smell, such as the salt of the sea, pine trees, or freshly cut grass? Walk yourself through the scenery as though you were on a path in that place.
- ❖ It doesn't even have to be a place. You can imagine anything that you personally find pleasant, such as the face of a loved one when they laugh. What are they wearing? What are they saying to you? Or, imagine your dog when he comes running to greet you as you walk through the door. Think about his warm breath and sloppy tongue as he attempts to lick you.
  - ~ Or it can be an object, such as a plain box whereby you open the lid and watch a red line of steam that goes into the box. That steam represents your temper as it's leaving

you. Allow it to come out of and then watch it enter into the box. Close the lid.

~ Or, sing your favorite tune in your head. Say the words of the lyrics as if you are singing them out loud. Listen to the tune as it plays out in your mind.

Can you see how your mind has turned away from the reality around you and moved to a calmer place?

Some people can simply count numbers in their head, but this doesn't work for everyone. For some, it needs to be a more complex set of thoughts, enough to take their mind away from the stressful situation. All it takes is a few seconds of visualization. Of course, it doesn't take you away from whatever you are experiencing. It is a coping mechanism to calm your thoughts. Perhaps it will help you walk from a volatile situation the next time you feel your anger rising.

Understand Your Own Body

Often, uncontrolled negative emotions can be associated with traumas of some kind. The accumulation of many negative emotions can lead to depression and anxiety too. When this happens, it's not unusual for such individuals to feel negative about themselves. Negative life experiences do undoubtedly lead to low self- esteem.

The only person who can boost your confidence is you. You should have other people to help you, but it's you who has to alter the way you think. To do that successfully, you need to get to know yourself well. You need to understand who you have become and why you behave the way you do. Here are a few pointers to help you achieve such a notion.

Learn what your triggers are that lead to you to feeling insecure and make you lash out angrily? Do you:

- ❖ Lose your temper with everyone? Or do think you seem to home-in on one person in particular, such as your spouse or even your children?
- ❖ Feel like you can't stop yourself from lashing out, even to the point of hitting someone?

- ❖ Feel sick, sweaty, or breathless before you get to the final stage of aggression?
- ❖ Hate everyone? The world, people, politics?

Only by interrogating yourself can you understand the truth of your nature. There's no point lying to yourself. You need to know the raw truth of what's going on in your head.

Write things down, such as in a diary. It's not a diary of your everyday events; it's more so you can log down your emotions. Also note what you were doing at the time when you felt weepy, happy, or even angry. You can keep it private or share it with someone you trust for advice.

See if you can recognize a pattern in your behavior. Do you feel irritable after eating a particular food? You need to find out when and why you became irritated. Ask yourself these questions for as long as it takes to get to know yourself.

- ❖ Learn to alter your thought patterns.

If you don't agree with someone's opinions, hold back on telling them. When you do attempt to discuss the matter, try not to be too blunt. Perhaps you could ask them to explain what they mean a little better as it's a topic that you're interested in, even if you're not. Try to see their point of view as they explain. This is the start of practicing empathy, understanding other people's point of view on how they see a situation. Try to perceive how they feel rather than focusing on what you might be feeling. It's is a tall order, and it will be hard to do if your own personality is typically introvert.

If you can practice this, it's a way to try and see the world outside of your own head. You don't have to start liking people; it's more about listening and observing them. Make a start on those around you, most especially those in your close social network.

❖ Learn to listen to other people.

The next time someone is describing something that happened to them, listen without speaking. Instead of coming back at them with your own similar experience, hold back on your words. Don't share your own encounter; instead ask them questions about theirs. Show an interest in them. By doing this, you're forcing yourself to look outwards instead of inwards at yourself. This will also teach you to become more empathic towards others.

❖ Don't dwell on your bad experiences.

This could be one of the hardest of all to do. Someone who has anger issues and other psychological problems often only remembers the bad events in their lives. Bad experiences seem to dominate their memories and ultimately their lives.

We all seem to remember those awkward moments. Sometimes we can look back and laugh at them; others are too painful and still hurt our feelings. If you dwell on the negative, it can only lead to depression and anxiety.

If depression sets in, then other mental health issues are often not far behind. Yet, how can you fight away bad memories that have left you scarred?

It's a difficult path to explore, and you will need help to sort out the muddle in your mind. It could be that medication can help. Make an appointment with a doctor or clinician, so you get the right meds.

How does someone pick themselves up when they're at rock bottom?

There is no formal answer because each of us has different coping mechanisms.

- ~ Some people may lock bad memories away and never allow them out. This isn't a particularly good coping strategy. Relapses will be common and often at the least unexpected of times. Better to get them out and dealt with by asking for help from a professional.
- ~ Others may give in and turn to alcohol or recreational drugs to help them forget. This only serves to make their lives worse and their depression deeper.
- ~ If you want a "normal" lifestyle, whereby you can earn money for your family and protect them, then it's important to treat your

emotions with respect. Seek help, and the professionals will show you many ways to cope until you find the right one that works for you.

To get your anger under control, you must take these first steps. Something is behind the reason why you feel the way you do. Admit that, and you can then seek to take steps to find help. Asking for help is never easy when your mind is not functioning clearly. To move on, though, you must swallow your pride and find help. With the right kind of guidance, you can make these changes gradually.

What though, can you do if you are the target of anger?

That's our next topic. It's never easy if the person you love is angry and abusive.

Chapter 9

DOMESTIC VIOLENCE

When we fall in love, most of us don't consider the possible negative side of our new relationship.

More often than not, it is women who suffer the most, but men do suffer too.

Poverty and Familial Violence

- ❖ Up until the mid-1800s, husbands had a legal right to beat their wives. It was not until 1920 that "wife beating" finally became illegal in all states in the US.
- ❖ In 2011, the US CDC (Centers for Disease Control and Prevention) recorded 4.8 million abusive attacks reported by women and 2.9 million by men.
- ❖ Intimate Partner Violence (IPF) reports that 3 in 10 women and 1 in 10 men, suffer various forms of violence by partners.

❖ In 2007, IPF reported that of over two thousand deaths related to partner violence, 70% were women.

These are staggering statistics and spread out as a worldwide problem too. Globally, 1 in 3 women suffers violent attacks by their partner.

Domestic violence can and does happen in all walks of life. Studies are showing that the risks are greater within the poorer sectors of society. Those on lower incomes tend to suffer more stresses and strains of life. It is more difficult for this sector to maintain a decent living standard. Recent statistics show that up to 20% of children will witness some form of domestic violence. Unfortunately, this vicious circle continues on through generations of families. Good parenting skills will be low on the agenda for adults who have suffered abuse and income difficulties themselves. These are the children more likely to mature with behavioral problems. Low Income can be closely related to the development of mental health issues, though not always.

Such results paint a bleak picture of life for those on a low income. Indeed, violence within the family is the third leading reason for homelessness, according to the US Dept. of Housing. For many, anger issues are prevalent in the marital home.

We all like to feel that we're protected by the laws of our land, but that doesn't mean you can pass the buck. If you are the cause of hurting someone because you can't control your emotions, you owe it to your loved ones to repair the damage. That has to start with yourself. You must make changes to your inner self, and that will resonate outwards like the ripples in a pond. Of course, this can only work if you want it to. Sadly, there are plenty of angry people who have no intentions of changing and will never try. Again, I reiterate, you have to want to improve your lifestyle for those you love and for yourself.

If you are an angry person, learn to curb your temper and improve your lifestyle. A more positive outlook can be brought on with a better diet, exercise, and relaxation methods. Introducing these good habits into your life will put you on the path to success, not only for you but your family and friends too.

This is why guides such as this one might help to highlight that you CAN make changes. Take the time to learn about the underlying causes of anger so you can find solutions.

Causes of Anger in Relationships

With the first blush of romance, most relationships are rosy and sweet. The hormones take care of that as the brain gets flooded with certain chemicals, such as dopamine. Yes, once again, it's the chemicals in the brain that drive our emotions, even in love.

Biological changes affect our moods, and with romance, the hormones make us feel good. Once you experience that true deep affection, it can be hard to live without that person in your life. Over time though, things can change in any relationship, especially if one of the partners has an anger management issue.

Relationship Melt Down

❖ Scenario 1

At the start of a loving relationship, both partners may class themselves as "we." They are a couple and tend to do things together. If one partner starts thinking more in terms of "me," than "we," it can be difficult for the other partner to accept. Arguments may set in with differences of opinions. This can cause tempers to flare and the ultimate act of lashing out by one of the partners. When that happens, it can often mean the end of the relationship. For the one who is still in love, despite the anger and abuse, it can feel almost like grief. How do they live without a person who has been in their life so intimately? They seem to want to forget the aggression and return to what they once had.

❖ Scenario 2

Two young people fall in love and end up married with children. It seems the normal thing to do. As they go through each typical phase together, they become burdened with more and more responsibilities. Getting a home together seemed exciting at the beginning. Once that home becomes a financial burden, all the fun disappears. Having a family was all they dreamed of. No one teaches us the burdens of becoming responsible for other people's lives.

Now the financial pressures are heavy. The young mothers often need to go out to work as well as manage the household. Couples spend less and less time together and begin to grow apart. As they do, it can involve an array of experiences, anything from having extramarital affairs to constant bickering.

In a relationship where romance has died, it can lead to making life-changing decisions. Often this can result in splitting up an entire family as divorce rears its ugly head.

It would be better if we could learn to recognize the early stages of a sour relationship, most especially if aggression becomes a factor. The last thing anyone wants is children witnessing their loving parents hurting each other. Nor will they want to take sides.

Signs of Stress

Stress can be a key factor in any relationship that is breaking down. The high emotional tension can easily lead to physical arguments. No one can foresee whether a sour relationship should battle on to see if they can get through and become happy again. Strong relationships still go through bouts of insecurity. If stress does set in, then you risk becoming ill. If you recognize such symptoms, then you must deal with healing yourself. If that involves separation for a while, then it's worth it before you become mentally ill.

- Tiredness
- Sleeping difficulties
- Unable to concentrate
- Making more and more mistakes
- Irritability
- Eating unhealthier foods for comfort
- Eating less as you have no appetite
- Having no time for yourself
- Not wanting to socialize
- Feeling ill, such as headaches, stomach aches, toilet problems, palpitations.

Acute stress from life's demands is exhausting. It's fine to experience short periods of stress; this is a part of living. If it goes hand in hand with an aggressive partner, then it can become more serious for your health. Chronic stress can make you short-tempered and hostile towards those you love. You may begin to smoke, or drink alcohol, or even take un-prescribed drugs to help you cope. If you never have time to do things that give you pleasure because all you want to do is get the day's routine over with so you can sleep, it's time to find out why. The trouble is that the stress doesn't go away if left untreated, and it may even turn into a deep depression. That's because you need to identify the root of the problem and tackle it.

There's no point if anyone tells you to snap out of it; the chances are you won't even realize you're stressed out. This is why it's important to recognize the symptoms we have discussed in this guide. If this sounds like you, then you need to take action.

Things can become even worse if you have an abusive partner or someone who is bullying you at work. Living with angry people only adds to a person's daily stresses. Resentment can turn into hatred. If you feel that the only time you have energy is when you both argue, it's the surge of adrenalin rushing through you. With that can also come an ability to behave recklessly. Such behavior could be something that might later be regretted.

How to Deal with an Angry Partner

Often anger that leads to violence is usually by a man who is the culprit. When it gets to the stage of violence, the man will be in no condition to listen or compromise as he puts fear into his partner. If you are the partner of such a person, here are a few immediate tips for the situation:

- ❖ Try to stay calm instead of lashing out with your own angry words. It might stop your partner from getting worse.
- ❖ Try to listen to the angry person's words and don't interrupt them. Let them have their say until they've finished. At that point, they are

completely immersed in their stress and are far more likely to lash out.

- ❖ Remain as positive as you can. If you can't say anything helpful, stay quiet. The last thing they need is someone acting hostile towards them. It may even trigger physical violence.
- ❖ Remember, there are two in an argument. If you can be the strong one and show compassion, you might be able to dampen their anger before it turns to violence.

If you are the victim of a violent relationship, you must assess your situation and make changes, particularly if you have children. Ask yourself:

Do you love your partner?

If so, can you convince them, when they are calmer, to seek help?

Violent people are insecure people. The quicker they become violent, the more insecure they are. They may not be comfortable with themselves. This means they'll have a terrible feeling of guilt and shame after their outbursts. The saying, "You always hurt the one you love," rings true in such cases. Most of us tend to feel annoyed at those we love the most when we get angry. In any relationship, though, it is going to take both parties to work together. Whether the angry person is your spouse, parent, child, or friend, here are a few tips to help them cope.

- ❖ The best time to reason with them over their behavior is when they are calm. That's the most likely time you will get through to them; they may even admit they know that they have a problem.
- ❖ Talk about how destructive and hurtful they can be when they lose all control. They need to know the raw truth to motivate them to stop their destructive behavior.
- ❖ Try to decipher if they feel depressed or suffer low self-esteem. If they do, then look at the options together on finding help.
- ❖ Assure them of your love and affection and ask them if you can go through it with them as you both find help together.

- Discuss the use of a "safe word" to let them know that you feel insecure about their behavior.
- Devise a regime together, such as how they can take time out for themselves. A good exercise regime can often help with discipline and anger control. A good diet will help too, as well as time to do things they enjoy.
- If the angry person in your life is already using alcohol or drugs, you must make the huge decision of whether you want that in your life. The added complication will delay them from being willing to get help. It can be done, though. Many an addict has pulled through because their loved ones helped them.
- If you are that person, then you seriously need to realize your problem. Again I repeat, addicts can and do pull through to turn their lives around. Coming off the alcohol or drugs will be no easy ride, but many of the addictive drugs may actually be the cause of the emotional moods. Once the body is rid of the poisons,

maybe a better future will be in sight and obtainable.

Problem-solving is about finding solutions, not about wading in pity. Every problem has a solution; you just need to find it. It may take years to resolve. But, if it means improving your lifestyle, it will be the best thing you can ever do for yourself and your loved ones.

Chapter 10

MANIPULATION AND ANGER

One major hurdle for those who feel irritable, annoyed, or angry for much of the time is that they are not willing to admit this. More often than not, they will be in denial. If you were to suggest as much to them, they would only become annoyed with you. Once they're left alone because they've pushed everyone away, perhaps then they may start to see that they have a problem. This is usually when it's too late, and much damage is done. Often with this type of personality, they feel that the problem is someone else's and not theirs. Angry people tend to block most of their emotions. All they are left with is the burning frustration of anger.

This can be even more difficult if they turn to alcohol or drugs to ease their troubled mind. Another factor at play may even be manipulation. If a person is manipulative, they force others to see to their needs and can even threaten them if they don't.

Narcissistic Personality Disorder (NPD)

These are people who want everyone to see them as good-natured. They will go to any lengths to become liked. Here is a guide of their typical characteristics so you can hopefully avoid them:

- ❖ Total lack of empathy
- ❖ Arrogant
- ❖ Self-centered
- ❖ Demanding
- ❖ Often talk with a loud voice
- ❖ Exploit others
- ❖ Seekers of admiration and like to be the center of attention
- ❖ Sensitive to criticism
- ❖ Always defensive
- ❖ Believe they are entitled to the best treatment for their own needs.

The main problem and there are many as you can see is that sometime a narcissist will often react with anger if things go wrong. They are highly controlling and may even view you as their property. Such possessiveness can lead to a horrendous type of jealousy on their part.

Devious Manipulation

- The manipulative, angry person can easily tap into another person's fears by discovering their weaknesses.
- Often, when you first meet such a character, they can come across as charming and generous to a fault. That's because they hide their aggressive nature at the beginning of a relationship. They will dig for your weaknesses and slowly take over your life.
- They may have no care if they hurt others because they lack the skill of empathy or even sympathy. Their world revolves around them and them only.

- Nothing is ever their fault, so they always blame others for everything that might go wrong in their daily lives.
- Often the victim of a manipulator is usually of a weaker character. Such people are more likely to have vulnerabilities.
- Everything they do is about their own gain and rewards.
- They have a great need to be in control as it gives them a feeling of power. They think of themselves as leaders.
- If they lose that control, they will most likely become angry and lash out.
- Such people don't care about social niceties; that's for everyone else, not them. Yet, they would be the first to complain if something happens that they don't like.
- These type of people are not good people to be around, and it will not be easy to get away from them if they do enter your life

Manipulation exists on many levels. Every time we see an advertisement, we are subtly manipulated by the sellers. These people, though, are not doing it for commercial gain, only for personal gain.

When an individual person tries to manipulate you, the chances are they are doing it for a sinister reason. They are selfish individuals who are out to control your life. Though they will never admit to it, they are suffering a personality disorder, and some are even extreme narcissistic, such as in the diagnosis of NPD.

Leaving a Manipulative Relationship

Do you live in a relationship with many flare-ups that make you feel afraid? It could be the reason you have made that all important decision of leaving. It is going to have its challenges, so you must be sure that is what you want. Your partner will try all sorts of tactics to stop you or get you back, and they will be painful for you to go through:

- ❖ They may change the entire situation around to make it look as though they are the victim, and you the perpetrator. One of their best tricks is to put you down as much as they can; it makes them feel powerful and in control.

❖ They will play on your emotions because they know your weaknesses.

❖ Gaslighting: It's when someone convinces you that you can't trust yourself. How they do this depends on the situation between you both. How they usually go about it is by causing you to feel confusion over time. Eventually, you will begin to question your own sanity.

❖ At first, you may get that dreaded silent treatment. Be thankful; their temper tantrums are much worse. Their pettiness will hold no boundaries as they try to make you feel guilty.

❖ You will need to plan your departure ahead of time, and if possible, find someone you can trust so they can help you, particularly if you are taking children with you. If your partner has made sure you don't have any friends left, then look up some help lines. At the very least you need someone, even a stranger, to talk through your escape plan because that is what it is.

- Organize somewhere to stay before you leave, even if it's only temporary.
- If your partner is prone to violence, then leave when they're not around. You could leave a note, so they know exactly what has happened. Or, leave nothing to give yourself some time to get ahead of the game.
- Ideally, you want to be a good distance away from them when they find out. They are going to try to get you back, using dirty tactics such as:
  - Behaving over-emotional and repentant, even to the point of breaking down to cry in front of you. It will be very dramatic in nature.
  - They may even threaten to commit suicide if you don't go back to them. It's a difficult situation to be in, but you must push ahead and ignore their threats.
  - When the anger comes, and it will, they will blame you. No doubt they will spread rumors and may even tell lies about you. Be prepared for the worse.

- You need to change all your contact information, such as replacing your sim card, so they don't know your new number. Keep your address a secret to start with, though they could come to your place of work and embarrass you. They may also try the sweet talk with flowers and gifts. It's all a show; try not to be taken in! If they insist they will change, remember you are walking on eggshells. The only chance of them changing is if they seek professional help. Should they agree to that, you would be best to remain separate for a few months to see if it happens.

Some manipulators are not as bad as others. If your partner rules your life and is violent with it, they are the worse kind. This may be the type of partner whereby you need to go to the police for a restraining order, so they leave you alone. Such dominating partners can turn into stalkers because they become obsessed with a person in their life.

It can be a difficult time for those who are the victim of a manipulative and violent person. If you feel threatened, then you must leave immediately, ideally when they're not around. You will most likely lose most of your possessions. Your safety and the safety of your children is paramount. Any loss is insignificant when compared to the possible violent repercussions. They may see you as a betrayer and look to seek revenge. You are going to need all the help you can get, so don't be afraid to ask. If you manage to get the perpetrator out of your life, you will become so much happier.

Chapter 11

THE IMPORTANCE OF EMPATHY

Whilst empathy is not something an angry person is likely to have, it is something that we should all strive to improve upon. If we all worked at becoming more empathic, the world would indeed be a better place.

Some people have so little empathy for others and the world around them that they don't even know what it is. Let's lay it out so that if they happen upon this guide, they have no excuse.

What is Empathy?

First, let's make it clear what it is not. Empathy is not the same as sympathy.

When you have sympathy for someone's situation, you most likely feel sorry for them. You might even pity them.

When you empathize for someone's situation, you feel the pain they are going through. You should be able to put yourself in their situation to understand their emotions. It's not about feeling sorry for them or pitying them. If you can feel their desperation, then you will also have a longing to alleviate their troubles.

What then has the empathy to do with anger? It is a form of therapy that could completely change your life around, should you suffer bitter, angry moments on a regular basis.

Empathic Anger Management (EAM)

This type of therapy does not replace your relaxation routine, such as breathing and visualizing exercises. It complements such techniques.

Aggressively angry people are ego-centric, as they believe that everything revolves around them. This can often result from a lack of support for their inner emotions. With no help for their bitter emotions, it means they have managed their emotions the best they could, their only supporter being themselves. In this situation, where unsupported self-help was the only option, it is like "The blind leading the blind." Someone who is already deep in negative thoughts cannot help themselves to climb out of such dark places. Instead, they spiral deeper within their negative outlook. After all, they can only see the world from their own perspective.

Sometimes we are so knee-deep in our own-self, that we become the center of that little world. By learning compassion and empathy, that inner world will open up. They will come to realize that there are many, many others who suffer too and some even worse than themselves.

It doesn't work for everyone, particularly for those with manipulative anger. This type of therapy will only work with someone who has a desire to overcome and control their regular angry outbursts.

Relationships

Any good relationship needs empathy, sacrifice, forgiveness, and learning to be non-judgmental.

For example, let's consider the relationship in a long-term marriage. It's unlikely that any extended relationship does not involve arguments in some form or other from time to time. Those who have been together for many years will confirm that it is:

- ❖ The art of compromising that glues their relationship together.
- ❖ The skill to understand what the other partner's needs are, even if they clash with their own.
- ❖ Making sacrifices, so others also find some happiness.
- ❖ About not putting other people down because they aren't the same as yourself.

These are caring characteristics that will seem alien to an aggressively angry person. Without empathy, compassion, and sacrifice from both partners, a relationship will become very one-sided. That's how the aggressively angry person will have lived their entire lives. They don't know how to balance a friendship.

The absence of knowing how to think about another person has left them with a rather selfish personality. The next chapter covers this topic in more depth because these are the fundamental characteristics of becoming a GOOD person.

Cooling Routine

The next time you feel your anger building up:

- ❖ Take those deep breaths we mentioned earlier.
- ❖ Listen to your thoughts before saying another word.
- ❖ Question yourself as to why you feel this way
  - ~ "Why do I think it's their fault?"
  - ~ "What have they done to make me feel that way?"
  - ~ "Even it is their fault, does it really matter?"
- ❖ Ask yourself, why they might have acted the way they have. Try to see the situation from the other person's point of view.

This set of questions won't work in all situations. It's merely a guide to show you how to think before you react? Stop for a moment before you lash out with anger and listen to the voice in your head. By forcing yourself to question your actions, you are immediately putting a brake on any aggression.

The best part of questioning your thoughts in this way is that you are coercing yourself to look at the argument from a different point of view than your own. You are working towards empathy, though you're not quite there yet. It does take time to learn this skill if you don't feel it in a natural way.

When you do speak, your emotions should be calmer. Try to make your words empathic, by asking them questions about why they feel as they do, or what they mean by their word? Don't ask in a sarcastic voice; you need to sound genuine.

To diffuse an anger outburst, all you need to do is take a little time to try to understand both points of view. This is not an easy task when in the middle of a row. Everyone wants to shout out their own version of the story. If this is happening, stop yourself from responding other than to listen.

- ❖ Take that deep breath.
- ❖ Think with compassion.
- ❖ Ask yourself questions
- ❖ Ask the other person questions and listen to their answers. Even if you don't like what they're saying, try not to speak. Instead, shift your mind to understand why they feel the way they do. This is where the non-judgmental part is useful.
- ❖ Wait until they have finished speaking before you reply.

Do this, and you will reduce the intensity of the situation. You might even have a quieter conversation as you listen to one another.

You've learned how to listen, but there's more to do yet. The next stage is a little harder because it is about learning to make sacrifices.

Sometimes, no matter how right you think you are, it might be better for everyone, including yourself, if you simply give in. That is the first step in making sacrifices. Though it might feel as if it goes against the grain of how you normally react when you feel angry. Yet, it should put a stop to the argument and ensure it doesn't escalate.

If you still feel infuriated inside, then you must force yourself to walk away from the situation. Continue to ask yourself questions instead of shouting in your head that it's all someone else's fault. Your internal anger needs to vent, go for a run, or just keep walking. Exercise is a great way to calm yourself down.

You must practice to keep this up whenever you think you are going to boil over with anger. You don't have to like what others are saying, but you do have to try to see their point of view.

Here's a situation on how an angry person can use empathy in a petty argument before he boils up with an aggressive response.

Case Scenario:

You're in the middle of a heated argument with your partner over the TV.

Take that breath through your nose, hold it, and let your stomach inflate. Let it go through your mouth.

Instead of using a loud voice to respond angrily to your partner, ask yourself if you understand exactly what the problem is. If you don't, then ask your partner calmly, "Explain why you're so upset with me?"

It could be that you're always in control of the remote and they're fed up with it. Whatever reason they give you now's the time to put yourself in their shoes. Would you like to live with someone who always chose what to watch on the TV? Would you like to be forced to always have to watch someone else's TV programs? I know this seems a trivial problem, but often the fiercest of arguments start from the smallest of problems.

This is the vital part, putting yourself in their situation to see if you could cope with it.

Next, you're going to have to make that sacrifice of admitting that you were wrong and work out how to share the TV.

By learning to become more understanding of others, you are substituting your anger for tolerance. That will make a huge difference in your life and for your loved ones too.

Chapter 12

THERE IS A GOOD SIDE TO ANGER

We've seen how anger is mostly considered a negative emotion. Yet anger is as natural as any other emotion, such as feeling happy or sad. Anger is not always an emotion to feel ashamed of. Sometimes, it is necessary to go through it so you can move on with your life. This is when anger can be positive. Anger can have a purpose in our lives.

Turn Your Anger Into a Useful Tool

❖ Boost of Confidence

If we want something really hard and can't get it, the frustration can cause us to feel angry. That doesn't mean it's bad to feel angry. It's an emotion that motivates us to try harder to achieve the object of our desires. Used in this way, so long as we're not acting with aggression, it's quite a useful tool to have. It means that we have set aside our inhibitions. That's because our thoughts are so focused on the injustice of not having what we need. This increases our confidence to allow us to negotiate better for ourselves. The anger stops us from feeling intimidated, so we're less likely to back down.

❖ Optimism

Research has shown a correlation between anger and optimism. One study was based on the differences of optimism in the genders. When confronted with the threat of a terrorist attack, 80% of the group felt angry, and they were men. However, they were more optimistic about possible future attacks believing they were less likely to happen. The other 20% of the group were women, and their reactions were different. They were more likely to feel fear instead of anger. They were also more pessimistic and worried about further attacks. Women believed if one attack had happened, then others could soon follow. The women had a more pessimistic risk assessment than men in this study.

❖ Protection

When we experience anger, it means that we are ready to protect ourselves. This can be useful in a relationship as it helps us express our feelings when someone has hurt us. Once again, we let down our guard and voice our opinions because we are experiencing anger. It's as if it gives us a protective shield making us stronger and more capable of defending ourselves.

❖ Anger in Grief

A time in our lives when we may be prone to a strange sort of anger is if we are unfortunate enough to suffer the loss of a loved one. Many mixed emotions will leave us in turmoil, and this can often turn to anger at the person you have lost. It's a time when we are emotionally distraught and will go through various stages of confusion. People deal with grief in different ways. It's important not to deny yourself the grieving process because it's essential to be able to move on. Without it, you may even feel angry with everyone around you. How can they all get on with their lives as if nothing has happened?

While you show your anger, you are physically connecting with other people, and that's a good thing. If you're not normally an aggressive person, then don't worry. It's unlikely that your anger will go anything beyond a snappy response. You need to feel this type of anger as it will lead to the next stage of the grieving process. Every stage plays its part so you can come out the other side with the acceptance of your loss.

- ❖ Self-Assessment

Often, when we have an angry episode, we can surprise ourselves by how domineering we can become. Afterward, as we calm down, it's not unusual to replay the scene out in our minds. Only then do we take notice of our own behavior and wonder if we went too far. This process causes us to self-assess our own behavior. We may reprimand ourselves for taking out our anger on other people. It's a form of self-improvement as you assess your own performance and seek to improve your own behavior.

- ❖ Avert Aggression

When people become angry and loud, it can be a signal to themselves and to others that the situation is becoming untenable. Sometimes, in the right situation, this can be a trigger for others to offer help to calm down the situation. It can act as a buffer from potential violence before an aggressive episode happens, so it serves as a warning. If you recall, we mentioned earlier in this guide that anger is not violence. It is an emotion, whilst violence is an action. In many cases when the noise of anger is heard, it's a chance for someone to help mediate the rising emotions. Sadly, this is not always the case as most of us only want to go in the opposite direction. For the trained ears and eyes though, it is an opportunity to intervene. If the perpetrators are not normally of an aggressive disposition, such intervention can prove useful.

- ❖ Righteous

This is a force that seeks justice where wrongdoings occur. In its raw form, anger allows us to seek justice by expressing our opinion. Under normal circumstances, we might not do this, so our anger edges us on. With this powerful force of strength, we protect ourselves to make sure no one takes advantage of us. It gives us a sense of boosted confidence.

❖ Therapeutic

Believe it or not, anger can be very therapeutic. That's because it helps us to discharge or vent our negative emotions. You might share angry words with a friend on how your neighbor played loud music all night long. By the time you've finished telling the tale, the chances are you feel much better. You are now unlikely to go and confront your neighbor with those same angry thoughts. Sharing your frustrations with a friend or loved one means you can vent without causing any harm. This releases your negative emotions in a safe setting. Anger can be constructive when controlled. If not controlled, then it can turn into rage.

By viewing anger as a normal healthy emotion, you won't feel the need to hide it. Don't deny yourself this natural emotion because it does have beneficial properties. Anger is an evolutionary adaptation that has its place inside your thoughts. It's not an emotion to fear. If you can control it, you can use it for the reasons outlined in this chapter. It's merely a means to express ourselves, so in a sense, it's a communication tool.

No one particularly likes conflict but it is a way of ensuring fairness where there is an injustice. Sharing anger is the best way to control such a situation. It allows us to inform others so they see our point of view on a situation. It helps us to get the "other side of a story" across. You might not have even seen that point of view had it not been for your own outburst. Being open and honest, as most of us are when in the anger-zone, it can help to prevent grudges from building up. When controlled, it can clear the air of any potential storm.

Ancient Chinese methods believed that each of the body organs represents an emotion. For anger, it is the liver and gallbladder. They concluded that if you can control your anger, these organs will function well. Whereas out of control anger will lead to digestive distresses as these organs suffer. Sounds pretty close to the truth!

Make your anger work for you by controlling it and utilizing its effects. By all means, use it to get the things that you want out of life. At the same time, don't abuse it or let it run out of control. Make good use of it by helping victims of injustices. That way, it becomes the tool of protection, which is what it should be. There's no denying that anger can cloud your judgment. That's all the more reason to keep it under control and make it work for you and not against you.

Chapter 13

BECOMING A GOOD PERSON

Changes on the Horizon

We've already looked at empathy, sacrifice, forgiveness, and learning to be non-judgmental.

Can you change your personality to include more of these positive characteristics?

Of course, you can, but there may be something that is stopping you. The wall of resistance could be your anger issues.

There is good news, though. If you can learn to understand the true concept of these characteristics, you're one step closer to making your anger issues disappear.

So, what exactly is a good person? Indeed, do any even exist on the planet earth?

Let's clear up the concept of a good person before we answer these questions. Everyone experiences anger because it is a human emotion. Chapter 12 showed us how anger does not have to be a bad experience. We can utilize this explosive emotion to improve our lives. A good person still experiences anger. What gives them the label of being "Good," is that they don't take their anger out on other people. A "good" person is a "caring" person. They can't possibly care about everyone in the world, though they probably do their best to care for nature too. They will practice all the good characteristics we have mentioned earlier in this chapter

By implying there are good people means that there must also be bad people. Sadly, this is raw the truth of our world, but that bad person does not have to be you. Even if you suffer violent outbursts, it does not mean that you are bad. If you know that you have hurt other people both emotionally and physically, then you are admitting your faults. You can still change. It can't happen overnight. As with any new skill, you must allow yourself a period of training.

Books such as this one are a great start in turning your life around.

Forgiveness

You already know the qualities of empathy. So, let's begin this guidance section on forgiveness.

Forgiveness is a major factor in being able to forgive others when you feel they have done you wrong. It's only when you can view a situation from another person's point of view as in empathy, that you can learn to forgive.

- ❖ It's crucial that you switch the focus from yourself, using those empathic skills. This is the only way to review a situation from someone else's point of view.
- ❖ It's also about learning to let go. Even if someone has done you an injustice, ask yourself, "Does it really matter?"

Of course, there are experiences in life that we simply cannot forgive. This is particularly so if we were children at the time or if it involves our loved ones. As we become adults, if something bad happened in our past, we find it difficult to let go. When we recall the bad memories, we are viewing them with our inner child's mind. It's not until we reach the ending of our teenage years that we can start to take control of our lives. Up until then, we rely on other adults to guide us. Some of us draw the short straw on the parents we end up with. In such cases, we don't have very good role models.

If you suffer recurring memories of bad experiences, you must consider some kind of therapy. Once you become an adult, you have the power to let go and move on. If you can't find that power, then get some help to overcome your problematic obstacles. The bad memories will never go away completely, but they'll become less important as an adult.

Forgiving the people who do you harm in your life is a difficult challenge. It is not the people in your past that matter any longer; it's those who you have in your present. Bad memories can make you an unhappy adult, but now you have the power to make your own decisions. Learn ways to cope with the past so you can move on to the future with a more positive outlook on life.

If you can achieve this, you can overcome your negative emotions and become a stronger person, the type of person who can learn to forgive others instead of resenting everyone who annoys you in some way. Some people will always try taking advantage of others. Instead of feeling angry with them, help them to understand what they did wrong. Allow yourself to forgive their transgressions and either walk away or help them.

Sacrifice

For example, imagine you are in a heated argument. You can see the other person is genuinely upset, but you can't stop yourself. You're becoming agitated because you know that your side of the story is the truth of the matter. Your anger is beginning to grow at their inability to see your side of the story. What do you do? The angry side of you wants to fight to the bitter end to get your point over. The empathic side of you will concede the argument to the other party. If you can do this, you have learned to sacrifice. Your mind stayed open to accept that it did not matter who was right and who was wrong. All that mattered was ending the upset cause by arguing. The result will allow the tension to dissipate.

As you learn such skills as sacrifice, you're also learning how to compromise. Compromising isn't about being right; it's about being sensible. To compromise is often to sacrifice because you will not be getting your own way. For an aggressively angry person, this would never be acceptable. They could not cope with other people winning them over. Yet, this is what you need to sacrifice for the sake of your health and the health of your loved ones.

If you are that person who explodes at every turn in your life, you can learn to sacrifice and compromise. Do this, and you can finally turn over a new leaf. There is much personal satisfaction in allowing other people to win the day. Even when you still believe that your point of view was the right one. Do this, and it means you have learned to sacrifice at the cost of your own feelings.

Being Non-judgmental

This may be the hardest skill of all for an aggressively angry person to overcome. Such people love to put everyone into boxes and categories. It gives them a sense of order in their inner turmoil. Their view of balance, though, is at the cost of judging others how they see them. Making up their own rules of how things should be. It's a form of personal labeling based on their own unbalanced judgment.

By being judgmental, we are assuming the outcome of everything should be the same.

For example, your neighbor gets arrested for shouting at his partner and disturbing the peace. You tell everyone that he deserved it because he's poor, fat, gay, black, or white. Yet, what gives you the right to come to that conclusion? You have judged the neighbor on gender, color, body build, or even on income. The truth is that the neighbor was arrested for none of those reasons. By assuming they were arrested for anything other than disturbing the peace, which was the truth, you are being judgmental. If you don't know the truth of a situation, then don't make assumptions.

For someone who is aggressive in nature, they will always believe that their version is the true one, even at the cost of incorrectly labeling a person by their own conceived and ill-judged opinions.

A good person would approach the partner left behind and help them with the situation. Clearly, our example family were already suffering difficulties. These will now have grown tenfold with one being arrested. They don't need labeling; what they need is help. If they don't want your help, then at last you tried. That is what you should aim to do with your life; try to help others with kindness and not with blame.

Chapter 14

MAINTAINING EQUILIBRIUM IN YOUR LIFE

Balance is the key factor when trying to attain a life of contentment.

There's no denying that the world can be a cruel place to live in. Some people can stagger from one bad experience to another, often with deadly consequences. It could be freak weather, a traumatic accident, or the death of a loved one, none of which we have any control over.

On the other side of the coin, we can also experience many amazing events such as the birth of a child, the love of a pet, finding a soul mate, or simply watching the sunset in a fiery, red sky over the ocean.

Given that we are bound to come across events we can't control, it makes sense to include as many positive ones as we can. That means avoiding bad experiences that we DO have control over.

If you're trying hard to control your anger but have a relapse, then it's not an excuse to let everything go. It may take a lifetime to turn things around and keep them that way. When things don't go the way you want them to, it's good to use the experience as a learning curve. You must learn that when you fail, the only option open to is to pick yourself up again and get back on track.

There will be days when you feel you can't keep battling your own personality just for the sake of those around you. Consider your transition like a dance, three steps forward, one step back. If you find you're unable to control yourself, at least turn away from the problem and scream up at the sky if you must. Do anything to stop yourself from confronting another person, whether you feel they deserve it or not.

Even calming down your own negative emotions doesn't mean that others will stop showing their anger towards you. Should such an episode happen, it may have the potential to unbalance you. This will be a provoking moment and one you may not be able to control. Think through how good it will make you feel if you can walk away.

Responding is the easy option; walking away takes courage.

Alternative Responding Mechanisms.

One of the best things you can teach yourself is that even when someone is in the wrong, it doesn't matter. The world will not end if you concede their point. Teach yourself what is really important in your life.

Here are some annoying situations with alternative responses:

Situation 1:

- If someone insults you or one of your loved ones.

Past Response

You would respond with aggression.

New Response

At the end of the day, their insult is only their personal opinion. If this person is not anyone important to you, why does it matter what they think? You have to learn to pull away from an aggressive situation.

Situation 2:

Your partner has left all the dirty pots and gone to bed. It looks like they expect you to do them.

Past Response

You would confront them aggressively, asking them with sarcasm in your tone if they thought an invisible fairy was going to do the dishes.

New Response

Why not do the dishes and say nothing at that point? When you have some time, create a roster of certain housework tasks. Present it to them with a genuine smile and not in an aggressive way. Explain that it might lighten the load to share things equally.

Situation 3:

A driver overtook you when there was no need because you're driving at the right speed limit.

Past Response

This would infuriate you. You'd start swearing and shouting in the car, or even open the window to do it, regardless of passengers.

New Response

STOP allowing things that other people do to annoy you so much. Yes, they were wrong, but there's nothing you can do about it once it's happened. If you get annoyed, you are running the risk of increasing your blood pressure as well as upsetting your passengers. Ask yourself, is it worth it?

Sure, it's so much easier to say what the outcome of a dispute should be when you're not in it, but that's the whole point. You have to learn to distance yourself from situations that cause your emotions to boil up. Pull your thoughts away from your negative responses. At worst, ignore the situation or walk away from it. At best, do your relaxation breathing and handle the situation with a more positive outlook.

Don't be a quitter!

Here are a few situations that might cause you to relapse:

❖ It's very hard to change a characteristic you've had all your life.

There's no denying that this is going to be difficult. Stopping a behavior that happens automatically without any real thought is a challenge in itself. That's why it's important to have a network of support. Although you are the only person who can force the changes, you don't have to do it alone.

This process of change should be done in stages. No one expects you to change on day one. Find a way of rewarding yourself every time you manage to control those anger outbursts. Don't forget that your reward is also in seeing those around much happier. They will love you all the more now that you're not losing your temper all the time.

- ❖ "They were getting on my nerves."

Concentrate more on your empathic skills when this happens.

Ask yourself why they are doing what they're doing. Search for the reasons and don't give up until you've calmed down.

Walk away, so you don't have to face-up to whoever is offending you. It's far better to walk away than start an argument that can only end up unbalancing your emotions.

- ❖ "It was their fault!"

Ask yourself, does it really matter who's fault it is?

What will that achieve?

It cannot undo any harm that's already happened.

Don't look for blame. Instead, look for solutions.

It has taken you a lifetime to be the person you are. Whatever life events you have lived through, they have made you into who you are. That's a lifetime of rich experiences. Take that knowledge and use it to strengthen your positive side so you can become a person who is content with their lot. Learn to push away angry thoughts. Write them down when they happen and use the notes to understand when and why you felt that way. Decide on a way forward to overcome your negative thinking patterns. Such thoughts and memories can only hold you back.

Chapter 15

Natural Healing

Natural remedies often complement prescribed medication. If you decide to try natural healing, you must research and check there are no clashes with any prescribed medication, although it's unlikely. If you're unsure, then consult your physician

There are various natural ways to help your psychological wellbeing, including:

- Deep breathing routine.
- Visualization.
- Peaceful walking with nature around you like in woodland or on a beach.
- Muscle flexing and relaxing throughout your body.
- Swimming and cycling.
- A healthy diet.
- A good night's sleep.

If you're considering cycling as a means for mental wellbeing, then avoid busy roads. That will not relax your mind. It's about finding ways to relax your mind and body as soon as you feel your anger or stress taking hold. If one thing worked for all, it would be wonderful, but it's not that easy. We all know that different things work for different people.

Also, consider natural herbal remedies. Whilst they may not be scientifically backed, many have been around for hundreds if not thousands of years. These are plant-based oils, seeds, and paste. Each has different properties to help with varying conditions. There are plenty of herbs that ease stress, anxiety, and depression. Here are a few that can be bought over the counter often as capsules, oils, teas, and seeds.

- ❖ St John's Wort has properties that help with mood swings.
- ❖ Valerian is helpful for a relaxing sleep, but you should not take it with any other sleeping medication.

- ❖ Passionflower also has a sedative effect, helping with both relaxation and sleep.
- ❖ Chamomile makes a great tea that you should consider using regularly. If you don't like the taste on its own, add some honey or lemon to it.
- ❖ Lavender's aroma is delightful. Studies have shown that inhaling its scent can help relax your mind.
- ❖ Lemon balm and mint all make for a lovely scent in your home. Mint tea will help with stomach problems, so will ginger tea.

If you don't want to consume these natural remedies, consider buying the oils to burn around your home. Essential oils are the best as they have little in the way of additives, so you're in safe hands when smelling these natural aromas.

If you're pregnant or take prescribed medication, you should check with your doctor that it is safe to use your chosen herbal remedies.

Here are a few more to add to your list of research to find the right one for you.

- Ginseng is great for giving you an added boost of energy.
- Garlic lowers your cholesterol levels, so get using it in your healthy cooking.
- Green teas will help your digestive system.
- Milk thistle is good for your liver, helping to repair damaged cells.
- Bilberries help with blood circulation. There is also evidence they can help with diabetes and cholesterol levels. Cranberry juice is good if you have a urine infection.

It can take a few weeks before you see any positive effects from herbal remedies. Start with a low dosage to make sure you don't have a negative reaction. There are many brands available, and it can be difficult to decide which products to buy. As a guide, you should look for the product with the highest active ingredients. Any quality product should also have an expiry date. Do follow the instructions, especially if you're taking other medication.

There are some plant-based foods that people can enjoy, but they can do us more harm than good.

- ❖ Coffee contains the caffeine that we crave if we need an energy boost. It's meant to help with concentration. The trouble is there are side effects if you use too much. You may become irritable or feel palpitations. If you have it late in the day, you might also suffer insomnia too. Too much caffeine is not good for your digestive system either. You can do without these problems when you're under stress. Try not to have more than around 100 grams of coffee on a daily basis. This means you can still enjoy the taste and benefits without it harming your health.
- ❖ Chocolate has also been in the media quite a lot lately. There are properties in it that can help to reduce stress levels and have a calming effect. If you are a chocolate lover, this does not mean

that you can eat large amounts. To benefit from the cocoa bean, you should buy dark chocolate that has at least 70% cocoa content. For instance, 100 grams will contain around 600 calories that also include sugars and fats. Look for bars of chocolate where coco is high on the ingredients list, and sugar is further down. If you see the words "alkali" or "ditching" on the label, don't buy it. It is a form of processing that changes the color and also reduces the beneficial effects.

- ❖ Red wine is another product that causes confusion. Whilst it is true that dry red wines contain some natural anti-inflammatory properties, it's not true that you can drink lots of it. All alcohol should be consumed in moderation. There's no reason why you can't enjoy the odd a 5 oz. glass of dry red wine a few times a week. This isn't a large glass, but it will be a nice treat with a few pieces of that dark chocolate.

Conclusion

Who would have thought that controlling anger could be so complex? Then again, humans are a convoluted lot. When it comes to human emotions, you must have realistic expectations. Nothing is going to happen overnight!

Our emotions form an intricate web of who we are as individuals. How we react to situations is dependent on what we have experienced throughout our own lives. Such experiences have helped to form our own personality. We must respect an individual's faults as well as their good side because it's taken them a lifetime to get there.

This book shows how anger can be managed. The perpetrator must be a willing participant, ready and willing to strive for a new lifestyle and outlook. It's not only for loved ones and friends that their anger needs to be controlled but also for their own wellbeing. The constant release of certain hormones that happens when a person is angry will have a long-term negative effect on their health. It can do no good to be continuously on alert, which is what they are, with anger.

We can become so wrapped up in our own negative thoughts that we are unable to see the world around us. It's not necessarily about being one with nature, but the outside world has much to offer. Many men love to go fishing and stand for hours on a peaceful, grassy embankment. They may not admit it, but they have found peace with nature. There are various aspects that will help anyone suffering from negative thoughts. If this is you, we will discuss how you can find a mindset of positive thinking. Only then can you appreciate the world and people around you.

Depression is a terrible, lonely condition. Those who have anger issues tend to suffer from low self-esteem, depression, and relationship issues. No one wants to be alone because we are social creatures at heart. Nor do we always want people in our face, but we do need some form of contact with our fellow human beings. It's vital not to see other people as your enemy. We all have their own demons to face, so we need to give each other space.

The advice in this book will not work for everyone. There are those who are happy being downright aggressive and manipulating. The rest of us should avoid such people. Often it can be that they have suffered irreparable damage and are unlikely to admit that they need help.

The key point of this book is that you MUST WANT to change. That is the main motivation and driving force to improving your lifestyle. None of us is the perfect human being; we all have flaws. It's when those defects involve hurting other people that you must open your eyes and admit that what you are doing is wrong. Inflicting pain on others, whether mental or physical, is the most selfish act a human can do. We have the intelligence to know better, and I'm not talking about academic intelligence.

Put your personal grievances aside and push on to overcome your negative thinking. There will always be someone who will annoy you out there. If you can become a better person inside your own mind, you won't even notice them. That's because you will learn to rise above the small things in life that have unbalanced you in the past. If you can turn your aggression into love, it will not be a miracle that has happened. It will be your own hard work to overcome those mental health issues that have dragged you down for such a long time.

Those of you who follow the advice in this guide and then implement the changes are set to become better people.

www.ingramcontent.com/pod-product-compliance
Lightning Source LLC
Chambersburg PA
CBHW031112080526
44587CB00011B/942